PINDAR

ANCIENTS IN ACTION

Catullus
Amanda Hurley

Cleopatra
Susan Walker and Sally-Ann Ashton

Horace
Philip Hills

Lucretius
John Godwin

Martial
Philip Howell

Ovid: Love Songs
Genevieve Liveley

Ovid: Myth and Metamorphosis
Sarah Annes Brown

Pindar
Anne Pippin Burnett

Sappho
Marguerite Johnson

Spartacus
Theresa Urbainczyk

Tacitus
Rhiannon Ash

ANCIENTS IN ACTION

PINDAR

Anne Pippin Burnett

BRISTOL CLASSICAL PRESS

First published in 2008 by
Bristol Classical Press
an imprint of
Gerald Duckworth & Co. Ltd.
90-93 Cowcross Street, London EC1M 6BF
Tel: 020 7490 7300
Fax: 020 7490 0080
info@duckworth-publishers.co.uk
www.ducknet.co.uk

A catalogue record for this book is available
from the British Library

ISBN 978 1 85399 711 2

Typeset by e-type
Printed and bound in Great Britain by
CPI Antony Rowe, Chippenham

Contents

All translations are the author's, based on the Teubner text of B. Snell and H. Maehler, Stuttgart and Leipzig 1997.

in memory of
George B. Walsh

Introduction

Pindar lived and worked in the first half of the fifth century BC. His home city was Thebes, in northern Greece. Alexandrian scholars fabricated biographies from misunderstood passages of his work, but almost nothing is known about his life.[1] He was said to have composed for multiple voices, having received early training as a chorus-master in Athens, and he seems to have travelled in the Greek peninsula and also to the western colonies when works of his were to be performed. A poet who worked for hire, he made laments and songs of lover-like praise, to be sung by a single voice at banquets, and also paeans, virgin-songs, dithyrambs and hymns meant for civic occasions and many voices. Fragmentary examples of all these survive, but only the odes made for familial celebrations of athletic victory have been extensively preserved, and these are the subject of this book. Commissions came from Rhodes, Thessaly, North Africa and Sicily, as well as from closer to home, and the number and diversity of his patrons prove that he attained his own wish, which was to be, among poets, what Hieron, tyrant of Syracuse, was among rulers – 'a manifest light, visible throughout all Hellas' (Olympian 1.116). True, Aristophanes, not fifty years after his death, could treat him as wholly out of date, a ragged poet from 'long long ago' (*Birds* 926-30), but his house at Thebes was nonetheless preserved, even though the city was sacked by the invading armies of Sparta and Macedonia. And as late as the second century AD, visitors to Delphi were shown a chair of iron inside the temple 'where, they say, Pindar sat when he came to sing songs for Apollo' (Pausanias 10.24.5).

Later antiquity classed Pindar as one of the greatest of Hellenic poets, recognised by both men and gods – the verses of his Olympian 7 were spelled out in gold letters in the temple of Athena on Rhodes. Still, since most of his work was meant for group performance where words, music and movement were transmitted to performers by oral instruction, only a small portion was preserved in written form. The privately commissioned victory odes survived best since copies were sometimes kept in family archives, and Alexandrian scholars collected and classified these as Olympian, Pythian, Nemean or Isthmian, according to presumed occasion. They also wrote commentaries which reveal that these odes for athletic victors were, to their ears, intemperate, boastful and shaped by professional jealousies. Following their lead, Horace, though he imitated Pindar's epinician style, made him an example of grandiose pomposity (*Carmina* 4.2.1-32).

By contrast, the poets and scholars of the Renaissance, when they discovered Pindar, heard a gloriously undisciplined singer, incomprehensible but delightful in his unlicensed daring. Ronsard admired his 'fureur' and his wandering digressions, creating a new verb when he boasted, 'First in all France, I have Pindarized!' (*Odes* 2.2.36-7). In England, Ben Jonson made an 'Ode Pindarick' that followed the epinician design, and Abraham Cowley, after translating several odes, characterised their style as exciting but dangerous for an imitator ('The Resurrection' 4.52-64, 1656):

Stop, stop, my Muse, allay thy vigorous heat,
   Kindled at a Hint so great.
Hold thy Pindarique Pegasus closely in,
   Which does to rage begin,
And this steep Hill would gallop up with violent course.
'Tis an unruly and a Hard-mouth'd horse,
   Fierce and unbroken yet,
   Impatient of the spur or bit,
Now praunces stately, and anon flies o're the place,
Disdains the servile Law of any settled pace,
Conscious and proud of his own natural force,
   'Twill no unskilful Touch endure
But flings the Writer and the Reader too that sits not sure.

The court of Louis XIV was taught by Boileau to admire the 'fine disorder' of a poet whose spirit 'seems to be led rather by the demon of poetry than by reason' ('Discours sur l'Ode', 1693). In the next century, this same notion of a verse that was lawless appealed strongly to Goethe and Hölderlin, but Pope had already added a drop of vinegar to his appreciation of the Theban poet ('The Temple of Fame' 213ff., 1715):

Across the harp a careless hand he flings
And boldly sinks into the sounding strings…
The champions in distorted postures threat,
And all appear irregularly great.

Voltaire, who perhaps knew the poet only in translation, went further and addressed the 'divine Pindar' with exhausted scorn ('Galimatias Pindarique', 1768):

Rise from your tomb, divine Pindar,
You who gave praise, in the past to

Horses that raced for the merchants of
Corinth or Megara; you whose natural
Talent let you say nothing with much talk;
You who gave artful shape to lines that
None understood and all were
Forever obliged to admire ...

Nevertheless Friedrich Schlegel, at the end of the eighteenth century, could praise Schiller as having a poetic style like that of Pindar, one that showed 'intensity of sensibility, nobility of thought, magnificence of imagination, dignity of language and authority of rhythm'.[2] And among the English Romantics, Gray likewise praised Pindar, not so much for his unreason as for a kindred quality, that of sublimity, and modestly introduced himself (in 'The Progress of Poesy' iii.3, 1757) as one who had inherited

Nor the pride nor ample pinion
That the Theban Eagle bear
Sailing with supreme dominion
Through the azure deep of air.

Shelley and Wordsworth were also admirers, and in her 'Vision of Poets' 312-17, 1844), Elizabeth Barrett Browning proclaimed herself dazzled by a

... bold
Electric Pindar, quick as fear,
With race-dust on his cheeks, and clear
Slant startled eyes that seem to hear
The chariot rounding the last goal
To hurtle past it in his soul.

Most educated Victorians, however, probably agreed with Dryden's old assessment: 'Pindar is generally known to be a dark writer, to want connection (I mean as to our understanding), to soar out of sight and leave his reader at a gaze' ('Preface to Ovid's Epistles', 1680). Tennyson could speak of 'a kind of Australian poet; has long tracts of gravel, with immensely large nuggets embedded',[3] and this judgement was restated in twentieth-century language by Ezra Pound, who called Pindar 'a damn'd rhetorician half the time ... the prize wind-bag of all ages'.[4]

Scholars of the nineteenth and early twentieth centuries produced editions and commentaries in which learning was sometimes matched by admiration, but when new studies of Greek metres showed that the 'licence' so much envied by the Renaissance poets was in truth an elegant exploitation of the traditional rhythms of earlier Greek singers,[5] poets forgot him and interest in Pindar came to be confined to a very small group of academics, not all of whom were admirers. Classicists newly concerned with questions of economics, politics and social justice were uncomfortable with poetry intended for aristocrats, works which, according to one Canadian scholar, reflected 'the lethal stupidity of a long dormant class'.[6] An eminent British thinker called him a 'toady' and asked, 'Can one divorce a great poet from his deeply felt but odious beliefs?',[7] while in France it was stated categorically that, for Pindar, 'the poet's job was to exalt the nobility and praise the rich landowners who were developing a luxury economy, spending large sums, glorying in their matrimonial alliances, and priding themselves on their horse-drawn chariots and athletic prowess'.[8]

Fortunately, the political and sociological concerns of the twentieth century did not prevent significant formal discoveries. Once the odes were compared with earlier works meant for group performance, their rhetoric, like their metrical practice, was seen to follow certain rules. Two eminent German scholars and one from the United States analysed poetic behaviour once judged to be random and disorderly and demonstrated that Pindar's sudden exclamations, self-exhortations, gnomic interruptions and seemingly unmotivated digressions all reflect traditional modes of praise.[9] What had seemed wilful self-indulgence or affected posturing could be recognised as part of the 'grammar of choral composition'[10] and heard in this way, the odes no longer showed that high contempt for sequence and transition that Cowley had so admired. They gained in unity but lost their lyric immediacy as they ceased to issue from the mouth of an impassioned poet who dared to break all rules. Indeed, the voice that said 'I' now seemed to belong more to the choral convention than to the poet Pindar, and some scholars supposed that, in spite of ancient opinion and internal evidence, the songs for athletes were meant for solo performance in a version of Pindar's own voice. This discussion is not closed, but most of today's Pindarists continue to hear these odes as sung by small bands of performers who might speak either for their formalised poet or for themselves, as representatives of the victor's celebrating relatives and fellow citizens.[11]

However strongly his own voice sounded in them, Pindar's engagement with the inception of these songs is plain. Hired by a triumphant athlete or some member of his family, he responded with words, music and choreography, but he could not simply follow his own inspiration. His song would come into being (and so have a chance at survival) only in performance – only if its patron judged it worthy to be brought out, like a fine wine, for the greater honour of celebrating kinsmen

and guests. As a purchased artifact it would reflect the wealth
and taste of an athlete and his house and it was made the more
valuable by the poet's professionalism – he could speak of a
song as 'cargo' sent abroad, and he once, with an ostentatious
metaphor, described his Muse as a bawdy-house keeper whose
silver-faced songs were sent out to work for profit (Isthmian
2.6-7). Alexandrian scholars loved to speculate about his fees,
but the significant fact is that the surviving odes were
preserved in family archives because they had met the requirements of this particular market. Each one, in performance,
must have given satisfaction to aristocratic victors and their
close associates. They were similar, in this way, to the masques
made for the English court in the seventeenth century, for
Pindar, like Ben Jonson, was obliged to please powerful
patrons, while working within a set of fixed conventions and
under sharply limited physical conditions.[12] The victory odes
spoke for a closed society as it contemplated its own well-
being. In order to understand the artistry of their poet – in
order to hear something of what their audiences heard – one
must consider the values and beliefs, as well as the realities,
that defined those who called themselves 'good men' (*agathoi*)
in early fifth-century Greece.

Praising a Victorious Athlete

Pindar's victory songs were usually performed before well-to-do all-male audiences brought together when an athlete returned from pan-Hellenic competition bringing a crown. The victor himself, or the head of his household, would gather as many male kinsmen and neighbours as he could manage, perhaps twenty or thirty, for a celebration in which music, poetry and dance, along with food and wine, would let him present his supreme good fortune as a permanent boon to be shared by the entire region.[1] Guests and hosts were meant to reach a state of mirthful joy, but this was no ordinary banquet. Sympotic companions, after delighting in each other's songs, or in the skills of acrobats and flute-girls, might rush out in an unruly band (a *komos*) to dance and sing at other men's houses, but the friends who drank to a crowned athlete stayed on their couches as a band of singing dancers broke in upon them. In this incoming troupe (also called a *komos*) there might be as few as six or, if this were a court occasion, as many as fifty boys or men, naked or nearly so, perhaps carrying garlands and accompanied by a lyre and sometimes by a pipe as well ('musical strings join with the babbling pipe', Olympian 7.11-12). They presented themselves as companions of the victor, revellers who followed the example of the victory-night rout (Olympian 10.76-8), and sometimes they claimed to bring news direct from the field of contest. Nevertheless, their odes were not imitations of actual shouts of victory, as Pindar reminded one audience (Olympian 9.1-5).

> The Archilochus chant –
> 'Victor triumphant!'
>   shouted three times –
> opened the revel when Epharmostos
> danced with his friends at Olympia,
> close by the Kronian hill, but today a
> volley of far-flying shafts like these must
> sweep from the bows of the Muses ...

Though the occasion was convivial, the victory dancers used 'shafts from the Muses' bows' – language, melodies and presumably movements designed by a poet and borrowed from religious choruses – because athletic competition was of interest, not just to men, but also to the gods of Olympus. Pindar did not use the solemn term, *choros*, for the singers of his odes, but the immortals were part of the audience that they addressed.

The victory songs were made and performed in the first half of the fifth century BC, a time when Greece was still a collection of small independent localities, in spite of the common threat of two Persian invasions. Separate regions, each defined by its major community, were still under the dominion of propertied families whose members performed particular duties, civic and sacred, as custom required. Challenged, or joined, by a rising middle class, such men were less powerful than they had been, but they still in many places held themselves responsible for the order and well-being of all who lived within the local borders, and this meant, in simplest terms, repelling mortal foes and attracting immortal friends. The local nobility customarily equipped armies and led them against common enemies, while they also sought divine favour by building temples and maintaining the traditions of sacrifice and feasting, and in this second area tradition pressed them to take part in athletic contests. The gift of highly trained human strength, publicly displayed, was always pleasing to the divine authors of safety and prosperity, and an outward show of power and pride remained an honorific duty among men of rank (cf. Aristotle, *Nicomachean Ethics* 4.2-3 = 1122b19-23a4).

Held in sacred places and dedicated to local heroes as well as to Olympian gods, organised games made an offering of men's ambitions – not just of muscle-skill, discipline and expense, but of the will to risk defeat, even death, in a sanctified trial. Contest was the 'work' of landed men – it was their job ever to court divine protection with displays of 'toil and expense, struggling in noble actions that are mired in danger' (Olympian 5.15-16), and such actions were also politically advantageous, for 'success gives a seeming wisdom in citizen eyes' (Olympian 5.16). Political structures had grown more complex in the late sixth century and the Greek view of the aristocrat began to change, but the noble athlete maintained his status. Even in the evolving city of Athens, Solon had to combat a general conviction that victors in the games deserved honours as great as those granted to warriors who fell in battle (Diogenes Laertius 1.55), and by grumbling about such notions – 'even an Olympic victory doesn't fill the treasury' – the popular satirist, Xenophanes, bore witness to their continuing prevalence (fr. 2 Diels/Kranz).

The so-called Crown Games – those in which Pindar's victors competed – drew athletes from all over the Greek-speaking world to honour Zeus at Olympia (sometimes

identified by the river Alpheos or by the Hill of Kronos),
Apollo at Delphi (associated with the springs at Kastalia and
with Mt Parnassos), Zeus at Nemea and Poseidon at the
Isthmus. Each festival had its own calendar but in any given
year at least one was held, always with the same essential
programme as athletes were compared in groups (running,
jumping, casting the javelin or discus, exercising equestrian
skills), or else tried in one-to-one conflict (boxing, wrestling,
or a rough mixture of both called the pankration); only the
complex pentathlon included trials of both sorts. Whatever the
event, however, contestants offered themselves as a kind of
sacrifice (at Olympia the footrace was contained within the
ritual sequence that offered a black ram to Zeus). Their combats
might replicate those of a local hero, and their organised strife
could be seen as a surrogate action, replacing a conceivable
divine battle that would bring chaos (see below, pp. 53-8, on
Isthmian 8), or ending actual strife. So, at Olympian 10.43-9,
Pindar reports the foundation of the Olympic games as the fulfilment of Herakles' vengeful war against Augeas:

> Zeus' brave son then brought his
> army with all of its spoils into Pisa, and
> there he measured a sacred grove for the 45
> greatest of fathers, fenced in the
> Altis as holy, and fixed the surrounding
> plain as a haven for feasts, with
> honours to Alpheos' ford and for the
> Twelve Ruler Gods.

For an athlete's offering of training and strength, grateful
gods gave a double return. In the actual moment of supremacy,
the victor knew an instant of contact with the power that had

fixed the outcome of his struggle (Pythian 8.76), and he seemed to stand, like the Peleus of Pindar's Fourth Nemean, in the presence of 'circling chairs where sat the rulers of sky and sea' (Nemean 4.66-7). Then, to his household, descendants and community there came a continuing and expanding gift called *kudos* – a talismanic renown that illumined all, like light from a star.[2] This indestructible prestige, the gods' response to a man's gift of expense and exertion, would enable both the victor and his locality in any future endeavour, while its lack would mean a shadowed or silenced ability (Olympian 5.14), and it was this intangible enhancement of power that, with his crown of bay, celery, or dried parsley leaves, the successful athlete brought back to his family, friends and neighbours. As a divine gift it was imperishable, but unfortunately 'past splendours sleep and mortals are forgetful' (Isthmian 7.16-20). Fame depended upon the tongues and memories of men and so required sung praise in witnessed performance (Nemean 7.11-16).

> When a man acts and succeeds, he casts a sweet
> subject for song into the Muses' stream, but
> even magnificent boldness is shadowed
> if praise fail! Noble deeds we can mirror
> only when garlanded Memory joins us in chanted   15
> fame-bearing song – due ransom for toil!

Furthermore, this empowering reputation, though granted to the community as well as to the victor, needed to be formally extended, and so the victory song became an act of genial reciprocity. On behalf of victorious hosts, it offered to share the gods' gift of *kudos* with equals and friends, and through them with the whole locality, while on behalf of those who received it, the ode voiced the praise that would repay such an exalted benefaction.

On learning of a victory, the head of the fortunate household commissioned a poet – the best-known were Simonides, Bacchylides and Pindar – to whom he gave details of family history and instructions about the scale and location of the intended celebration. He wanted an entertainment that would please his guests while it gave the kind of praise that his house deserved. When it was finished, the ode was either brought by the poet or delivered, with notes as to music and dance, by a messenger, and once it was accepted singers were chosen, usually from the victor's age-group – the best voices and bodies to be found in the neighbourhood. (According to Xenophon's Sokrates, a handsome boy was even more handsome when dancing, *Symposium* 2.15.) As the group was rehearsed, by the poet or by a local trainer, an echo of its song would reach the local population, but the single full performance took place, as a rule, in private, and always showed certain fixed characteristics. The dancers, once they had entered, sang in unison, their song made in stanzas that were usually grouped in pairs by the interjection of a slightly different metrical unit called an epode. (There might be just one such 'triad', but usually there were more – thirteen, in the monumental Pythian 4.) Moving, in most cases, among guests who had finished dining, and taking account of the placement of couches and the size of the room or courtyard, they might perform as a rank or in the round, walking, prancing, jumping, crouching, kicking low or high to front or back, sometimes separating into twos (facing one another or side by side), always with eloquent gestures of arm and hand (Chamaeleon, at Athenaeus 14.629b). These traditional movements, known to all educated males since childhood, were probably repeated with the repeating stanzas, but whatever their choreography, the performers could never be spread very wide, nor could their bare feet be too active. The victory dancers were always 'stepping light', as one group proclaimed (Olympian 14.17), because the sense of their song was more important even than the delight that their movements might bring to the eyes of an audience.

Seeing their own sons, nephews, brothers and neighbours in the *komos,* the guests heard Pindar's words as coming, on a primary level, from familiar mouths. Those words, however, were shaped by traditional choral practices as well as by the poet's taste and intent, and the occasion maintained a certain formality though, paradoxically enough, a pretence of spontaneity was primary among the conventions observed. Everyone knew that this was a well-rehearsed performance designed by an expensive poet, but effective praise of god or man had to come from the heart, and often the singers entered as if simultaneously struck by a need to celebrate – 'Someone must go to the gates of his father to rouse up a revel for Kleandros and for his youth ...!' (Isthmian 8.1-4). Sometimes they dramatised a sudden resolve, shouting to one another, 'Make a revel of melodious song!' (Isthmian 7.20), or 'We'll dance in a *komos,* away from Apollo and Sikyon and off towards new-built Aitna ... so make a sweet hymn!' (Nemean 9.1-3). As if engaged in a joint act of improvisation, they might speak as individuals or as a group and often they pretended to arrive with news – 'I come with a musical message, report of an earth-shaking four-horse car that gives triumph ...' (Pythian 2.3-5), or 'I want to announce Telesikrates, blessed man, as shield-bearing Pythian victor ...!' (Pythian 9.1-3). Occasionally they would suggest that their task was beyond them, confiding, '... but the fair deeds that followed are more than I can recount. I come, o Muse, as keeper of victory revels for Pytheas ...'

(Isthmian 6.57-8), or again, 'my tongue is too short to tell all' (Nemean 10.19). With an assumption of modesty, they could ostentatiously scold themselves, singing, 'Spurn that tale, o my mouth!' (Olympian 9.35-6), or 'Drench that boast in silence!' (Isthmian 5.51). At other times they might proudly draw attention to their own cleverness, as when a Sicilian troupe summed up its opening triad with a metaphor from the javelin-throw: 'I grasped the moment that offers much, nor did my cast prove false!' (Nemean 1.18).

The singers of a victory ode might seem to speak to themselves, to the victor, or to men in general, but the fiction of spontaneity gave primacy to the immediate audience. Silent spectators were in effect drawn into a kind of interaction with the performers, dramatising the fact that together the two groups represented the local community. So, proclaiming an inspired uncertainty, dancers could ask themselves and the gathered guests, 'What god, what hero, what man shall we sing?' (Olympian 2.1-2), or, addressing the city, 'Which ancient glory, o blessed Thebe, brings most delight to your heart?' (Isthmian 7.1-2). In another case, they challenged their listeners, 'Speak out! Who killed Kyknos, killed Hektor?' and so evoked a silent but unanimous cry of 'Achilles' from the surrounding couches (Isthmian 5.39). They might warn of a coming synopsis ('I know a short cut!' Pythian 4.248) or indulge in provocative asides ('But have I gone wrong?' Pythian 11.38; 'Do I boast out of turn?' Pythian 10.4; 'Let him who listens report whether I sing off-key!' Nemean 7.69). All of these tricks, adapted from the locutions of public choruses, emphasised the fact that epinician performers, like the singers of paian or hymn, spoke for, as well as to, the community that was their audience. An Aiginetan group made this explicit when, indirectly addressing the local hero, they

23

announced: 'I touch Aiakos' sacred knees in behalf of this city he loved, and of these townsmen' (Nemean 8.13-14).

On certain occasions the celebration seems to have been held on sacred ground (the singers of Nemean 3 bring their praises to a terrace below the Apollo temple in the city of Aigina), but even in domestic surroundings Pindar's victory singers sacralised the occasion. To begin with, they used the somewhat arcane Doric dialect that flavoured many songs of cult (this pompous language, plus the beauty of the poetess, caused Pindar to be bested by Corinna in a song-contest, according to the later report of Pausanias, 9.22.3). In addition, the members of the *komos* ritualised their performance by naming their own actions as they occurred; like the magician who chants 'I cut!' as he cuts his herbs, youths from Aigina might sing, 'I stop my light feet and take breath', as they did just that (Nemean 8.19). And finally, with more solemnity, the singers might voice invocations and prayers. An ode could begin with a call to an otherworldly power, like the 'Zeus, Driver of Thunder!' that inaugurates Olympian 4, or dancers might invoke local female powers, as with the address to Semele, Ino, and Leukothea at the opening of Pythian 11, or the call upon the Graces that begins Olympian 14 (1-5).

O song-famed Charites – you who
take as your portion a place where fine horses
roam by the streams of Kephisos,
you who are queens of wealthy Orchomenos,
patrons of Minyans of old – listen to me as I pray!

Prayer could also mark the end of an ode; twelve of the forty-three surviving victory songs are sealed with formal pleas for continued success, six of them addressed to Zeus, like the lines that preface the end of the ode made for Diagoras of Rhodes (Olympian 7.87-9).

> O father Zeus, Atabyrion's* lord,
>   honour the law of Olympic song, and
>
> ep. honour this man who invented the
>   virtue of fists!

*mountain on Rhodes

Compare the opening of the last triad at Olympian 5.17-21, with its formal plea, 'O saviour Zeus, high in the clouds, with a dwelling on Kronos' hill ... I come as a suppliant breathing through Lydian pipes to ask that this city wear deeds of famed prowess as ornaments!'

In the presence of immortals thus summoned, the chorus would address its simplest task, the ritual chanting of the victor's name along with names of victorious brothers, uncles, fathers, and ancestors, as well as names of places where crowns had been taken. In addition, particular prizes – tripods and golden cups (Isthmian 1.19), or woolly cloaks (Olympian 9.97) – might be recorded as enduring evidence of glory. One ode, Olympian 13, counts more than sixty crowns, then concludes that it would be 'easier to number the sands of the sea' (line 46), while Nemean 6.58 notes the present victory as the twenty-fifth claimed by the family of its boy-wrestler. And in the brief performance of Nemean 2 the family name is sounded four times in as many stanzas as a full count of victories is made (18-25).

> ... Timodemids! Four crowns they brought from
>   tow'ring Parnassos, won in the games, eight
>   more from the folds of lord Pelops' domain,

gained among people of Korinth, while seven were
taken in contests for Zeus, at Nemea, and
others past number at home! Citizens,
dance for that god while you hail Timodemos'
   well-famed return –
raise a sweet song and celebrate him!

Names, when chanted by many voices, took on a magical
permanence, so that the victor's service to the gods and his
community was repaid, not just with an immediate 'salve' of
healing mirth and jollity (Nemean 4.1-5), but also with
'genuine glory, the wage of fine actions' (Nemean 7.63).

Formally bestowed, such praise sealed the union of the
victor with his community, as the wine in a wedding-cup
joined two households when a father gave his daughter in
marriage (Olympian 7.1-7), but the singers also performed a
second and even more significant function. In the moment
that he gained supremacy, the victor had felt the touch of an
otherworldly power ('a daimon provides it, tossing one up as
he pins down the other', Pythian 8.76-8) and a version of this
transforming contact was now to be offered to his guests and,
through them, to the surrounding population. A common
experience of divine presence was, after all, among the aims of
most Hellenic rituals, where it was achieved through choral
mimesis of a mythic moment, and Pindar employed the same
means. Every major victory ode contains a passage in which an
act of divine intervention is presented as immediate experience, then interrupted (usually by a gnomic saying), so that the
impression of an otherworldly presence remains sharp.

A singing group did not narrate, nor did its members indi-
vidually take on roles, but the *komos* could sketch a mythic
situation, bringing certain details into sharp focus as it

imitated and emphasised the actions described. No background was needed, nor any steady chronological development, as the singers fixed upon single moments in which marvels occurred, frequently offering palpable objects to the listener's imagination – a cup 'bristling with gold' brought to Herakles by Telamon (Isthmian 6.40), or the bright shield of Alkmaon, with its snake device, as perceived by his buried father (Pythian 8.46). Otherworldly power might be given a form almost visible, so that listeners seemed to see Zeus' golden snow, as it fell on Rhodes (Olympian 7.49-50), the enormous eagle that visited Telamon's hall (Isthmian 6.50), or the three silvery snakes that attacked the new-built wall of Troy (Olympian 8.37). Often the event was labelled as a marvel, the response of the audience directed by inner witnesses represented as struck with wonder (like Aietes, as he looked on Jason's success with the fire-breathing oxen, Pythian 4.238; cf. Herakles, at Olympian 3.32; Artemis and Athena, at Nemean 3.50; Amphitryon, at Nemean 1.55). And finally, the speech of heroes and gods could be directly replicated, just as it was in cult songs, so that, for example, young Argive singers could let their audience hear the voice of Zeus, as he marked the triumph of Pollux with a promise of life for his dying brother (Nemean 10.83-90).

'If, fleeing death and hateful old age, you would
    come by yourself to Olympus, to
dwell there with me, close to Athena and
    Ares whose spear is black, that

ep. lot may be yours! Or, if instead you would
    fight for your brother and share with him
equally, you may for half of your time take

27

breath in the underworld – then, for half, in the
golden houses of heaven.' Pollux knew
no indecision, but first opened the eyes,
then freed the voice of
    Kastor, the bronze-belted warrior.

Thirty-six of the forty-three surviving Pindaric victory
odes employ depictions of this sort – fragmentary mythic
episodes actualised through sensual detail and offered to each
spectator as his own fleeting experience of divine power.
Danced delivery encouraged a particular style: often the
subject was identified, perhaps with a proper name or
geographical location, then illustrated in a series of quick
glimpses which might or might not be organised chronolog-
ically. Such effects were almost theatrical, but unlike tragedy
and epic, choral song was not bound by relevance or logical
sequence; moments from unrelated tales could be mingled,
and results could be glimpsed before causes were sketched.
Nor were these scraps of legend didactic or moralising,
though they might contain a potential threat; listeners were
asked, not to imitate the figures evoked, but only to appre-
hend them for a brief instant of awe and empowerment. In
one case, familial victors from the past were made present
(one binding his fists with sharp thongs), then transformed
by a capping glimpse of Achilles as his 'raging spear' struck
Memnon (Nemean 6.34-44, 50-3), but otherwise a mythic
moment was chosen. Sometimes the depicted scene was a
close reflection of athletic victory, as in an ode for a boy
wrestler, which led its listeners to feel, through a Peleus
matched with Thetis, first the onslaught of an otherworldly
power, then its inconceivable transformation into a god-
given prize (Nemean 4.62-8).

Fire all-devouring, claws of bold lions,
dread biting edges of sharpest teeth –
these Peleus endured, then

married that high-throned Nereid girl!   65
He saw the circle of chairs where sat
rulers of sky and sea, offering
power and gifts for his race!

A Syracusan audience watched as a newborn Herakles
focused Zeus-given strength in tiny fists that strangled a pair of
serpents (Nemean 1.44-5), and the guests of an Aiginetan
merchant seemed to hear the gasps of dying lions that were
carried off by a six-year-old Achilles (Nemean 3.46-50).
Elsewhere, a mythic figure might be glimpsed as he received an
empowering gift – from Poseidon, a gilded chariot with
winged team for the winning of a bride (Olympian 1.87), or
from Zeus, a warrior son not yet present in his mother's womb
(Isthmian 6.42-54). At Syracuse, guests first watched an abandoned baby given food by a pair of silver-eyed snakes, then
heard Apollo grant him the power of prophecy (Olympian
6.45-7, 60-70). Apollo's voice also sounded at a celebration on
Aigina, as he promised Aiakos an ultimate Trojan victory for
his descendants (Olympian 8.42-6), and the family and friends
of an Aiginetan boy heard Themis give the gift of order to all
creation by interrupting the strife of Zeus and Poseidon over
the couching of Thetis (Isthmian 8.35-7).

'This you must stop! Let her lie in the bed of a mortal,
then let her watch as her son dies in battle, though he be
equal to Ares in strength, to a fire-bolt in swiftness of foot!'

For an extended and complex example, one may look at the central portion of a song made for an extraordinary Corinthian athlete who had won Olympic crowns in both stadium race and pentathlon. The chorus praises the city as mother of inventions, and lists the victor's many successes, then turns back to the legendary glories of Corinth, to arrive at last (by way of the Trojan war) at Bellerophon and the tale of how Athena gave victory into his hands in the shape of a golden bit (Olympian 13.59-92).

> ... Greeks trembled when Glaukos
> came up from Lykia boasting of rule,   60
>   broad lands, and a palace in
> Peirene's city*, derived from his
>
> ep. father who, there at the nymph's spring,
>   tried to tame Pegasos, child of the
> snaky-haired Gorgon. He suffered much until
> Pallas the Virgin stepped as reality
> out of his dream, holding a golden   65
> bit. She spoke: 'Do you sleep, o Aiolid
> king? Take this horse-charm, offer a bull to your
> father, Poseidon, and show this to him!'
>
> 4. As he lay sleeping in shadow it seemed that the   70
>   Maid of the dark shield uttered such words. He
> leapt to his feet, found the marvel that
> lay on the ground by his side, and
> joyfully sought out the prophet,
> Koiranos' son, to tell him the tale, beginning to end – 75
>   how, by the seer's own counsel, he'd

slept for a night at the goddess'
   altar and how she,
daughter of Zeus of the thunderbolt spear,

gave him a curb made of gold for his steed. He was
ordered to honour the vision and, when a heavy-hoofed
bull had been slain for the Maker of   80
Earthquakes, to raise up an altar for
Hippic Athena. Immortal
power means easy completion, even of
   deeds beyond hope or sworn oath.
Mighty Bellerophon took up the gentling
   charm, reached to
stretch it around the animal's jaw, then   85

ep. mounted that winged horse and,
   bronze-clad, made play with his weapons!
Riding his steed, he sent arrows from chill
pockets of air, killing the female
Amazon horde, Chimaira the
fire-breather, and too the tribe of the Solymoi.   90
His fate I smother in silence; the
horse claims a stall in Olympian stables!

*Corinth

Created by familiar poetic means, fixed by sensuous detail,
and enhanced by sacred associations, scenes like these left
hosts, guests, and singers momentarily exalted, but such effects
held a certain danger. The fame of the victory now shared by
all had become inextinguishable – it would 'forever spread its
undimmed radiance over land and sea' (Isthmian 3/4.59-60) –

and this meant that all present had, like Bellerophon, known an honour that might be misused (they had, like the Tantalos of Olympian 1.55-6, tasted feasts they might fail to digest). The Pindaric victory ode gave its celebrants a fleeting contact with immortality, and this meant that the same ode had to placate the gods with compensating gestures of mortal diminishment. The singers' frequent suggestion that their work might be flawed (e.g. 'Did I make a wrong turn?' Pythian 11.38) helped to deflate possible divine resentment, but the true antidote was administered in gnomic statements about the limitations of humanity: 'As time rolls on, life shifts its course, tossing up this and that – only the race of the gods goes unscarred' (Isthmian 3.18).

Proverbial wisdom held that all men were alike in their dependence upon higher powers, and all the odes were generously sprinkled with pronouncements of this sort, probably delivered in a conventional wise-speaking manner. At the beginning of Nemean 6, guests who celebrated an Aiginetan boy were reminded that, though they resemble the gods, 'we men cannot know, by day or by night, what destiny marks as our course' (lines 6-8). Interrupting an account of triumphs, introducing or following an episode from legend, or anywhere else in their song, the dancers would warn all present that 'Man's joy springs up in a moment, and in a moment falls' (Pythian 8.93), or perhaps that 'gods ever provide two evils with each single good' (Pythian 3.81-2). The lesson of mortal limitation is repeated again and again: 'Men's hopes surge high, then sink, as all journey through waves of illusion' (Olympian 12.6-7), 'No man is, or ever will be, without his due share of trouble' (Pythian 5.54), or 'Rich and poor together move towards death's boundary' (Nemean 7.19-20). The pillars of

Herakles several times figure man's definitional limits, with insistence upon the foolishness of anyone who should think to cross this boundary (Olympian 3.44-5; Nemean 3.21; Isthmian 4.12-13). Every form of human success is held to be open to reversal from above, just as winds will always change (Olympian 7.94-5; Pythian 12.31-2), but this truth is especially applicable to the present occasion. Each man must remember that 'the mortal limbs one wraps in splendour will in the end be clothed in earth' (Nemean 11.15-16). Even one who, having taken a major victory for himself, then sees his son crowned at Delphi 'will never walk the bronze floors of heaven, though among mortal joys he may visit the furthest ports' (Pythian 10.22-9).

These constant reminders of mortality allowed the whole gathered party to be brought back in the end to the superb realities of the actual occasion. The performance might end with a resumption of praise for the victorious household (the final triad of Olympian 13 mentions sixty-six major familial crowns, with others beyond counting), or (less frequently) with a prayer for further glories ('may he take armloads of unmatched garlands from Pytho and Elis!', Isthmian 1.66). Final lines might also reassert the powers of song, recognise a trainer, or describe a particular action to be performed as the celebration reached its end (Olympian 9.111-12 directs that a crown be placed on the altar of a local hero; cf. Nemean 5.53-4). But whatever the form of its closing, each ode dismissed a victor with a 'heart turned towards mirth' (Isthmian 3.10) and an audience unified and ready to join him and the dancers in a truly unrehearsed revel. All would now proceed into that condition of vinous hilarity that Pindar called *euphrosyna*, 'best healer of toils' (Nemean 4.1-2; cf. Pythian 4.129; Pythian 11.45; Isthmian 3.10; Olympian 14.14).

2

Celebrations for Boys

Pythian 10; Nemean 7; Isthmian 6; Isthmian 8; Nemean 3; Nemean 8

In well-to-do Greek families of the early fifth century BC boys were educated among the women until they were about seven years old – so, in Pindar's Nemean 3, the six-year-old Achilles is still in the house of Philyra, the mother of his protector, Chiron. After he had begun to live in the men's part of the house, a boy might be taught to read and write by male tutors and, together with others, instructed in music and choral dancing. Most important for many, however, was the child's introduction to the recognised contest sports, which also came at this time – Aristotle would later complain that the traditional physical training began much too soon (*Politics* 1338b-39a). Practising in a local hall, field, or gymnasium, boys learned to run and jump and to throw the discus and javelin, and soon they were introduced to the aggressive one-on-one arts of boxing, wrestling and the pankration (a fight in which only biting and eye-gouging were ruled out). Brothers, cousins and neighbours of roughly the same age would work together under trainers who supervised every move and marked any foul with the rap of a long stick. Then, when most of his new teeth had come in, a boy might begin to compete in local games and, if he were successful there, family pride would begin to push him towards one of the pan-Hellenic festivals. Pindar notes a presumably rare case of parental timidity that kept one youth from major competition (Nemean 11.22-3), but for those with athletic ability life would as a rule centre upon competition until they were eighteen and ready for military training. The ideal Greek boy put his strength and his skill on trial and made a show of his exploits because youthful virtues were meant to be displayed, not 'hidden away in a snake's lair' like a child's discarded toy (Isthmian 8. 70).

Courage and a rage to win were thought of as innate, but the fine points of regulated contest sports had to be demonstrated and practised. If a boy showed promise, especially in boxing, wrestling or the pankration, a private trainer might be found and this man, himself an erstwhile contender, would sometimes become a member of the household, directing his pupil's diet as well as his exercise, and going with him to competitions to coach him on the spot. At Olympia a trainer might, like a father or brother, stand beside a youth at the altar of Zeus Horkios as he swore not to break any rule (Pausanias 5.24.9-10), and a coach could be fined if he in any way opposed the instruction of the judges. In a few cases, the trainer was a kinsman; the Aiginetan Pytheas, himself a boy victor, trained his younger brother for the pankration, or as Pindar put it, 'he set the course for Phylakidas' blows' (Isthmian 5.59-60). Usually, however, the coach was brought from outside, even from another city, and he was well-paid because this kind of expense focussed the ambitions of a family. If his pupil was successful he might remain for several years as a major guide from childhood to adulthood, a Chiron to his pupil's Achilles, but also a 'charioteer' who guided the youth's hands and his strength (Nemean 6.65-6; cf. Isthmian 3/4.89, where the trainer is a 'helmsman').

Four such coaches were honoured by name in songs made

for boy-victors. A certain Orseas who had trained a young Theban pankratist was 'sprinkled with revellers' joy' at the end of Isthmian 3/4, and a boy of Western Lokris was urged by his *komos* to honour Ilas, the man who had made him a victor (Olympian 10.17-21):

> Let
> Hagesidamos, Olympian victor in boxing
> offer his best thanks to Ilas –
> as, to Achilles, Patroklos did!
> One man, by sharpening
> natural valour, may with god's   20
> help turn another towards
>   gigantic glory.

The Athenian Menander was hailed with a pun when a chorus reminded its boy-victor of what he owed to his coach – 'Know this! Toil's sweet reward comes to you through Menander's high fortune! It's right that a builder of athletes should hail from the city of Athens!' (Nemean 5.48-9). Most eminent of all, however, was another Athenian, Melesias, who received a long passage of praise at the core of an ode made for the thirtieth of his pupils to bring back a crown, Alkimedon, a young wrestler from Aigina (Olympian 8.53-66).

> If my song treats the fame that Melesias
>   won among beardless youths, let
> Envy not cast its rough stones! I shall   55
> tell of his similar glory
> garnered at Nemea, and of a
> prize taken there among men in the
> pankration. He who knows by experience

teaches more easily – not to consider is   60
folly and untried hearts are too eager.
This man explained, better than others,
which moves, what style would
bring a man home bearing coveted
   fame from the sacred games.
Now, for this trainer, Alkimedon   65
takes a thirtieth victory prize!

Any major competition meant leaving home for a consider-
able length of time; at Olympia there was a thirty-day training
period on the site, during which one was required to abstain
from any 'slothful or ignoble act' (Philostratus, *Life of
Apollonius* 5.43). Male relatives and friends would accompany
a boy and his trainer, along with age-mates who might or
might not compete. Once at the site, a contestant was quali-
fied or disqualified by examining officials – Pherias of Aigina
was barred from wrestling a Olympia in 468 BC on the grounds
that he was too young (perhaps under ten), but he came back
four years later and took the boys' crown (Pausanias 6.14.1).
Isthmia and Nemea were the best places for athletes not yet
fifteen years old because in those contests a special class of
adolescents – the *ageneioi* or 'beardless' whose chins were
downy but not yet rough – drew off the older and larger
youths.[1] Everywhere, however, the years just before eighteen
were the finest, for at this age one stood at the top of the boys'
category but did not yet have to meet adult competitors.

For Greeks of Pindar's time, departure from home, seclusion
among those of one's own age, adherence to special rules, and
performance of a final exploit, followed by a joyful return, was a
sequence of actions that suggested an advance towards a changed
status. Athletic competition had an initiatory quality among

boys, and especially when the event was one of direct combat – the choice of twelve of the sixteen youths celebrated by Pindar. Whatever the contest, however, those who took crowns were given, on their return, a temporary reception at the symposium, the private club of mature masculinity. There, feasting together, Greek men defined themselves as drinkers of wine, makers of song, admirers of youth, and citizens who welcomed the Muses and chose, when at leisure, not to think about war or violence (they were 'men skilled as warriors who scale wisdom's peak', Olympian 11.18-19). Free women had no place in their dining halls, nor did boys of citizen standing, except in this extraordinary moment when a youthful victor was brought in with his companions for formal praise among his elders. He would, for this one evening, share the couch of his father or some other male relative, to watch as a troupe of his age-mates performed the sort of song that might have praised a man.

For a prize-winning boy, the victory celebration enacted an advance towards the condition of masculine adulthood, and this is made plain in an ode wherein the homecoming of a crowned boy wrestler is contrasted with that of contestants who failed (Pythian 8.81-93) .

5. Four bodies you fell upon, meaning dire harm,
   nor were returns such as yours
   granted to them by the Pythian judges!
   Finding their mothers, no sweet
   laughter brought joy – they came, dodging their   85
   enemies, skulking up alleys,
   gnawed by misfortune's sharp bite.

He who was dealt fresh success, meanwhile,
   soars in soft luxury,

raised up by hope and floating on pinions of   90
manliness, thoughts aimed
far beyond wealth!

A loser hid with his mother, while a winner was brought
with his friends among admiring fathers and uncles. In such
company the city became his 'mother' (Olympian 9.20),
Herakles his companion (Nemean 7.86), Zeus his divine
sponsor, and this step towards maturity was witnessed and
affirmed by those who performed the boy's ode – friends,
cousins, erstwhile opponents and future rivals. If the victor was
under fifteen he was praised by piping voices and dancing
bodies still childish in form, while a 'beardless' youth would be
celebrated by dancers who 'showed the first ripeness so
pleasing to Aphrodite' (Isthmian 2.4-5, cf. Pythian 6.1, 'we
work Aphrodite's fields'). Whether their chins were downy or
smooth, however, dancers and victor together were given a
brief taste of what their wine-drinking elders most valued – a
confident male unity enjoyed in elegant leisure and conducive
to order and good counsel. This was the condition that Pindar
called Hesychia (Nemean 9.48, cf. Pythian 8.1-5).

Sixteen of the surviving Pindaric odes celebrate victors who
were between twelve and eighteen years old. In scale, these songs
are comparable to those made for men (though none is as long
as Pythian 4, none as short as Pythian 7), and they are formally
and functionally like the songs for adults. They sanctify the
occasion and attach the immediate victory to the boy's household, emphasising the transfer of fierce ambition from one
generation to the next ('Nobility bred in the bone shines out by
nature in father and son!', Pythian 8.43-5). At the same time the
glory earned by the young victor's innate power is extended to a
community that voices its grateful return of 'ungrudging praise'

(Olympian 11.7). The generic choral devices are employed – the prayers, self-descriptions, fictions of spontaneity, and also the bits of proverbial wisdom which, however, will have suffered a slight loss of solemnity when offered by childish voices. (Indeed, there is something like open provocation when, after singing of 'love's holy sweets' at Nemean 8.4-5, the chorus of dancing boys reminds its admiring audience that 'Best pleasure comes when a timely choice, made from the finer desires, takes its prize!')

Nevertheless, there are certain differences. In songs for boys, the powers summoned by opening invocations are most frequently female (Hora, goddess of youth, Nemean 8.1; Klotho, Isthmian 6.17; Semele and Ino, Pythian 11.1-2; Hesychia, Pythian 8.1), and these figures are often strongly marked as maternal: there are calls to Eleithyia, goddess of birth (Nemean 7.1), Theia, mother of Helios (Isthman 5.1), Mother Olympia (Olympian 8.1), Thebes, 'mother of mine' (Isthmian 1.1), and to 'Mistress Muse, our mother' (Nemean 3.1). The youth of the boy victor is on display and he is praised by his friends as handsome, desirable, shapely, a marvel to look at (*kalos*, Olympian 8.19; cf. Olympian 9.94; Nemean 3.20; *eratos*, Olympian 10.99; *morphaeis*, Isthmian 7.22; *thaetos*, Pythian 10.59; and note Olympian 14.22-9, where reference is made to the boy-victor's long hair). A pankratist from Aigina, 'fair in himself', 'matches his beauty with deeds' (Nemean 3.19-20), and a young boxer from western Lokris is said to 'wear the same youthful bloom that once (with aid from the Kyprian) kept Ganymede safe from death' (Olympian 10.103-5). Again, these songs may take on a playful air of juvenility, indulging in child-like exaggeration (as when a Telamon just come of age is said to have 'taken Troy', Nemean 3.37), or unfavourably comparing an imagined rival chorus with the players in a common children's game (Nemean 7.105). There can be teasing bits of arithmetic – 'twelve four-horse chariots, each with two drivers' (Nemean 4.28-30), or 'ten-thousand roads each one hundred feet wide' (Isthmian 6.22) – the effect being to integrate celebrating men with the victor's young companions as all work out the sum. And finally, occasional passages of trainer praise set the boys' odes apart from those made for men since, whatever the actualities, only youths boasted of having been prepared and directed by another athlete.

In their essential function, however, the songs made for boys matched those for men, bringing a touch of permanence to the victory and its celebration. With the exception of two that are very short (Olympian 11 and 14), all of them made contact with the realm of the timeless by recreating snatches of myth and offering them to the sensory experience of their audience. These scenes did not teach moral lessons or hold out heroic examples for imitation, as the Victorians expected them to do. Instead, they induced a sense of immediate extra-human presence, while they pictured the inherited strength, divine favour, or individual boldness necessarily present in any achievement of supremacy. Under such influence, all who took part, whether young or old, seemed to advance with the victor into an altered condition.

A transformation of the immediate feast is wrought with rare directness in Pindar's earliest ode, made for a boy of Thessaly. Composed probably in 498 BC when the poet himself was only about twenty years old, Pythian 10 simply superimposes a doublet scene from myth upon the present actuality so that time and the timeless are momentarily indistinguishable. The song is in some ways atypical, for it was made at the request, not of a relative, but of an admirer – a certain Thorax, chief of the Thessalian nobility. (His brothers, mentioned at lines 69-70, would in ten years' time, according to Herodotus 9.58, give strong support to Mardonius as the

Persians invaded Greece.) Young Hippokles had brought back a crown from the Delphic 400-metre footrace, and his celebration was to take place, not in his father's house, but in the ruler's hall, where he would be sung, not by boys but by men. In these special circumstances, Pindar made those men begin by asserting the Hellenic identity of their northern homeland (1-3) and the Delphic origin of Hippokles' crown (9-10), after which they gave special praise to the boy's father, also a crowned athlete (12-16), who was probably present.

1. Happy is Lakedaimon, and blessed is Thessaly!
   Both take their kings from Herakles' line,
   he who was bravest in battle! Do I
   boast out of turn? No! – Pelinna* and
       Pytho demand it, as do the
   sons of Aleuas†, eager to rouse up a song from   5
   men who will celebrate Hippokles.

   He likes the flavour of contest! Parnassos' hollow
   speaks out his name to its neighbours as
   best in the boys' two-stade race. Among
   men, o Apollo, the end is sweet when a   10
       god calls the start! By your design he
   took his success, while a temper inborn made him
   follow the path of his father, a

ep. victor two times at Olympia wearing the
    armour of Ares – Phrikias, judged at the games
    held beneath Kirrha's steep rock‡ as   15
    best in the footrace! May
    Fate grant to their latter days proud
    riches that come to full flower!

2. Not scant is their share of the joys known to Hellas –
    may envious powers send no reversal! One whose   20
    heart knew no pain would be god, but
    happy and worthy of hymns from the
        poets is he who triumphs with
    strong hands or feet, takes crowns with boldness and
    power, then lives on to see his young

    son wear a fated Pythian wreath as his   25
    due! Heaven's bronze vault is not
    open to him, but whatever glories we
    mortals may touch – these he explores to the furthest.

*Thessalian capital city   †Thorax and his brothers   ‡at Delphi

With Phrikias and his boy established as an example of superlative good fortune, the song moves into the mythic mode, announcing its shift with a wise saying that emphasises its departure from the limitations of the real world. The audience is to be taken on an impossible musical journey to the legendary land of the Hyperboreans (28-54):

        Travel by
    ship or by foot, you'll not find the magical
    path to those halls beyond Boreas where   30

ep. Perseus, leader of men, once entered and
    dined, welcomed by hosts who sacrificed
    hundreds of asses! Apollo
    ever delights in their
    feasting and worship and laughs at the   35
    towering lust of the beasts,

3.   nor does the Muse shun such rites.
     Everywhere maidens in chorus,
     lyre-songs, and cries from the pipe swirl out, as with
     bay-leaves of gold bound in their hair, citizens joyously   40
        celebrate. Not illness nor wretched
     old age can mingle with this sacred race –
     they live without battle or toil,

     safely escaped from the rulings of
     Nemesis! Led by Athena and
     breathing out boldness, the son* of Danae was   45
     welcomed by this blessed crowd after he'd slaughtered the
        Gorgon and carried her
     head with its serpentine locks – petrified death –
     back to the islanders. I find no

ep. marvel achieved by the gods to be open to
     disbelief. But hold oars, drop the prow   50
     anchor into the depths as a guard against
     rough sunken rocks, for a
     hymn at its finest flits like a
     bee from one tale to the next!

  *Perseus

Fresh from his Delphic victory, young Hippokles has just made his appearance among the feasting friends of Thorax when the dancers transport the entire company into this parallel world. All find themselves in the (unreachable) halls of feasting Hyperboreans, where, fresh from his victory over the Medusa, a young Perseus makes his appearance. Both occasions, the actual and the mythic, are filled with the music of pipe and flute, and so today's Thessalians seem to share the experience of a 'sacred race' that has escaped the 'rulings of Nemesis' (41-3). They too seem to hear the laughter of Apollo, as provoked by the obscene play of the sacrificial asses (33-4), but almost at once the Hyperborean scene is invaded by an earlier moment from the same myth when, led by Athena, Peleus had entered the halls of his enemy, Polydektes, carrying as his victory crown the Gorgon-head that turned all the guests to stone. The momentary effect is to endow the present boy-victor with a monstrous threat, the present audience with a paralysing fate, and the singers insist on this danger with their ostentatious self-admonition – 'But hold oars!' (51). They stop before going aground and avoid their self-made poetic reef by giving an erotic aspect to the favourite of today's host. After this performance, the boy's comrades, his elders, even young girls, will all be stunned like the people of Seriphos, for they will find Hippokles even more wondrous to look at than nature has made him (55-9).

4. I hope, as men of Ephyra
     pour out my sweet-sounding voice on
     Peneios' banks, to make Hippokles yet more
     fair in the eyes of his comrades and elders, while for
         girls still unwed he becomes a
     theme of compelling concern!   65

The concept of desire then leads to a general gnomic state-ment about fulfilment – the necessity, in a shifting world, of grasping what has been granted, of transforming ambition into happy action. This the poet has been able to do, thanks to the generous arrangements of the lord Thorax (64), and all present may do likewise, as they grasp the further pleasures of the cele-bration offered by their generous host (59-end).

45

Loves tease different
minds in different ways, but   60

whatever each may pursue, if
caught, let him hold it as his dearest
care, for no one can tell what the year's turn will bring!
I trust the welcome of Thorax who, graciously eager,
    yoked up for me the four-horse
car of the Muses and, friend to friend,   65
willingly leads out this leader.

ep. Gold, when tried on a touchstone, is bright –
as is an upright mind. His fine
brothers we praise, who support and
strengthen the customs of   70
Thessaly, where governance rests with the
best men, a cherished inheritance.

Thorax had evidently asked that in Pythian 10 formal praise
for the father should be mixed with a tribute to the beauty of
young Hippokles but, as might be expected, fathers are
strongly present in most of the songs for boy-athletes. The
qualities that made a winner were thought of as inherited, the
victory potential passing from father to son (or in certain families appearing in alternate generations), for it was part of an
ancestral fate. Victory thus proved a boy's descent, joining him
more closely with his parent (even as Orestes' victory over
Klytaimnestra and Aigisthos joined him with the avenged
Agamemnon in the mythic example proposed by Pythian 11).
Seeing one's son a victor is good fortune strong enough to
attract divine envy (Pythian 8.71-2), and the news of such an
event, carried to Hades, can rejoice a dead father who rests

there (Olympian 8.77-83, cf. Olympian 14.20-4), while a living grandfather gains in strength (Olympian 8.70). Especially in the case of a child's victory, the entire familial line is implicated and this notion was given a grand mythic form in Olympian 8, where spectators listened as Apollo explained to Aiakos the role his descendents would have in the ultimate fall of Troy (42-6).

> 'Troy will be taken where your hand, o
> hero, has wrought – so speaks this vision
>   sent me by loud-thundering
> Zeus, son of Kronos – nor
> apart from your children shall these walls be
>
> breached, but they will fall with the first and the
>   third generations!'

That the victor is the creature of his ancestors was also the guiding theme of Nemean 7, an ode that critics have found unnecessarily difficult. Made for Sogenes, an Aiginetan boy victorious in the pentathlon, this song announces at the outset that familial fate is to be its subject, for it begins with an opening call to Eleithyia, a goddess of birth ordinarily invoked only by women:

1. Eleithyia, throne-mate of deep-purposed Moirai,
       daughter of powerful Hera, listen, o
           maker of children! Without you,
       no one sees light and the kindly dark,
       or takes his portion of supple youth from
   Hebe, your sister! Yet men do not draw their first breath as 5

equals, but each is yoked to a fate apart.
Marked, thanks to you, for pentathlon prowess,
Sogenes, son of Thearion, must now be sung!

There follows a meditation on the function of praise in the preservation of deeds, with Homer's unfair treatment of Odysseus and Ajax cited as an example of how, with their 'winged devices and lies', poets can lead men astray (20-3). Eventually, however, a true assignment of glory will be made, and in illustration the singers cite Neoptolemos, the son of Achilles. He is introduced abruptly as one honoured by a god; next, his importance as conqueror of Troy and king of the Molossians is established, and then – in a supremely efficient final line of the song's second triad – he is killed, after which his permanent fame is established (30-50).

... But Hades' sea-surge will   30
break over all, whether seeing or blind, while
    honour waits only where god
nurtures the fame of the dead. As an
ally he came to the navel of full-breasted earth* –
he, Neoptolemos, lies there in Pythian soil! – after he'd
sacked Priam's city, where Greeks too had   35
laboured. Sailing towards home, he missed Skyros,
wandered, then touched on the Epirote shore.

ep. Briefly he ruled as Molossian king – an
    honour yet held by his line – then, with
    spoils he had taken from Troy, he went   40
off to the god and there, in a
fight over sacrificed meats, a
    man with a knife cut him down.

3. His Delphic hosts felt deep grief, but such was
    Destiny's claim. An Aiakid lord was to rest in the
        god's ancient grove through all time,
    close by the walls of the temple, as   45
    guardian presence when hero-processions
    passed with their many gifts. For justice, three
    words will suffice: not false is the witness
    marking the deeds of sons sprung from
    you, o Aigina, and from great Zeus!   50

˙Delphi

Ignoring the magnificence of the hero's final resting place,
critics of the present day see this episode as a deliberate outrage
that Pindar has wrought, for one reason or another, upon his
own victory song. Neoptolemos, they say, was the Greeks' first
great war-criminal, guilty of sacrilegious cruelty at the fall of
Troy, and justly punished for his atrocities by the god Apollo.
Consequently he can have no function in the praise of young
Sogenes, and must appear here because the poet is pursuing
some misplaced purpose of his own.[2] This view, however, while
it honours the gossip of Hellenistic scholars, forgets the perfect
warrior and ideal son that Odysseus describes in the *Odyssey*
(11.505-37). What is worse, it further ignores the dynamic of
Pindar's actual song and also the fact that, to be preserved, the
piece must have pleased Thearion, the host and father who set
this performance before his friends for their entertainment.

The overall movement of the ode is from infancy to adulthood – from the goddess who oversees the transfer of paternal
qualities at birth to a hero who is the companion and guide of
Hellenic youth in its passage to manhood. The paternal hall
stands close to a precinct of Herakles, and the singers move

Sogenes into that hero's formal care by way of a direct plea (94-101):

> O blessed one,
> you have the power to bend Hera's lord* or the   95
> Maid with grey eyes†, while often you strengthen a
> man when there seems no salvation! Clothe both his
> youth and his lustrous old age with a steady life-force,
> weaving for him a long tissue of
> happiness, and may his sons' sons forever keep –   100

ep. even surpass – this present honour!

*Zeus †Athena

Within this large pattern, the achievement of a destined Aiakid glory through the translation of a young warrior from death to perpetual honour offers a suitable mythic analogy, since a change of status always involved dying to the old condition. True, the death of Neoptolemos was in some other versions an Apolline punishment imposed for an act of sacrilege (the hero's attack upon a suppliant Priam at the taking of Troy), but Pindar's telling, with its anonymous killer and its immediate shift to perpetual glory, refuses any such suggestion. Neoptolemos in this telling is the son who, endowed by his father with heroic qualities, finishes what his parent began and fulfils the splendid fate of an Aiakid lord (44). Thearion can be proud to find his analogy in Achilles, Sogenes to be linked with this son, and according to the singers themselves, this bit of myth will also be pleasing to a particular guest – one who has come from Epiros, where Neoptolemos' descendants still rule ('the man from Achaia … won't fault me!', 64-5). An evocation of his predecessor's death and ultimate glory thus becomes a hospitable gesture towards a visitor from far away. And finally, according to the chorus, the choice of Neoptolemos has the virtue of novelty. Had they pulled in the same old tales that other singers favour, their song would be as tiresome as the repeated chant from a noisy children's game (102-5).

> Not with rough words have I drawn Neoptolemos
> into my song – this I deny – but ploughing the
> same field three or four times ends in futility,
> as when a child barks out to the others,   105
>   'Korinth was Zeus' son!'

Inherited strength was of primary importance in victory, but it had to be confirmed by divine sanction, and this truth was demonstrated in a scene brought to life by the singers of Isthmian 6. This time the commissioning father, Lampon, had himself known no athletic success and Pindar, in praising his son Phylakidas, chose a mythic moment in which a divinity joined with a splendid father in the making of a yet more splendid son. The song as a whole is a prayer to Zeus, asking an Olympic victory for this household where sons have already taken two crowns – 'Grant us a third libation of honey-voiced song, to be poured out on Aigina honouring Zeus as Olympian saviour!' (7-9). The fulfilment of this plea would let Lampon 'anchor his ship in the furthest harbour of bliss' (12-13) and the song closes with proof that, as paternal caretaker of family and city (65-75), he is worthy of such an end. Meanwhile the central part of the song has concerned itself with another prayer, and the engendering of another triumphant son.

51

The mythic scene of Isthmian 6 comes into being around
the figure of Telamon, who is defined as father of Ajax as soon
as he is named – 'none are so blighted as not to have heard of
... Ajax, Telamon's son, or of that father!' (24 ... 26-7). He is
an Aiakid parent whose deeds were overshadowed by those of
his son and the song tells how his wedding celebrations were
interrupted by a Herakles who calls upon Zeus for divine
interference (35-56).

Come to enlist his Aiakid friend,   35
he found a wedding and as he stood, wrapped in his
lion's skin, Telamon brought him a cup bristling with
   gold, that Amphitryon's
spear-bearing son* might be the first to
pour a libation of nectar. He took it and
stretching his masterful hands towards the skies,   40
uttered these words: 'If, father
Zeus, you ever have listened with
   favouring heart to a
prayer of mine, o hear me now as

ep. my solemn words ask that you
bring in due time from Eriboia a child – a bold   45
son for this man and for me a fated
friend! Make his body impervious,
   like to this hide that enwraps me,
won from the beast that I killed in the first
contest at Nemea, and let his heart be the
   same!' In answer, the
god sent an eagle, ruler of birds, and   50
   he felt the touch of a sweet inner joy

3. as, like a prophet, he further proclaimed, 'The
    child you desire will be yours, Telamon! Call him
    Aias the mighty after this eagle-sign† –
        he will be fearsome
    everywhere men work at war!' This said, he
    sat, and the fair deeds that followed are   55
    more than I can recount …

    *Herakles   †eagle = *aietos*

The words of one hero bring about the engendering of
another hero in an almost exclusively masculine process (the
bride is no more than a name, Eriboia, 45) that has its climax
when the eagle of Zeus penetrates mortal space. Dramatically
placed at the end of the central triad, this is the marvel that
caps the scene, and Herakles' response (50) is designed to
command that of the audience. Like him, all are to know an
almost erotic pleasure at the coming of this bird – a pleasure
that 'scratches' or 'tickles' according to the verb that the poet
has chosen. Handled in this way, the scene from Telamon's
wedding party captures the divine force in the act of making a
victor and hero who will surpass his father.

Another example of divinity's role in the creation of a victor
is depicted by the chorus of Isthmian 8, where the engendering
of a hero has cosmic reverberations. In this case the young
athlete, Kleandros of Aigina, has crossed over to the Isthmos and
to Nemea for contest and is now literally passing from one status
to another, for he is leaving the class of the 'beardless', to
compete in the future as an adult. His victory, in the pankration,
has come soon after the battle of Plataea (479 BC), where men
from Aigina took part in the defeat of the Persians, and where
something like 1,500 Greeks were killed. In these circumstances

a boy's victory in a mock battle cannot be met with an outburst
of unmixed joy, especially since a paternal cousin, a boxer named
Nikokles, has recently died. It is not easy to celebrate, as the
chorus at once admits, each singer miming an attempt to master
his unreadiness. Nevertheless, this youthful pankratic victory
may signify not only the end of Kleandros' boyhood but also the
close of a desperate time (1-15):

1. Boys, for Kleandros
        and for his youth, someone must
    go to the grand outer gate of his
    sire, Telesarchos, to rouse up the
    revel that offers a glorious ransom from toil –
        payment for victory taken at Isthmia
    and for his Nemean dominance!   5
        Yes, I am asked, though I
    sorrow, to call on the golden Muse.
    Freed as we are from heaviest griefs, let's not
    cherish our losses and cares nor
    orphan ourselves of crowns! Stubborn evils have
        come to an end, so
    let's meet together in sweet civic joy even
    after such pain! Hung as a menace over our
    heads, the Tantalos stone has been   10
        shifted away by some god –

2. task beyond bearing
        imposed upon Greece. But fear,
    left from the past, rises to halt my
    strong inspiration. Best keep eyes on one's
    feet, for a treacherous destiny hangs over all,
        ready to twist the path of one's life! Yet –

even such fear has its cure, where   15
    men know of Freedom!

With the word 'freedom' (*eleutheria*, 15) tongues are loosened and the singers remind themselves of legendary ties between their poet's home city, Thebes, and the island of Aigina, where Aiakos and the Aiakids are honoured as local heroes. This lets them raise the curtain on a meeting of the gods that determines, first, that a cosmic monster shall be left unengendered, then that the magnificent warrior, Achilles, shall have a divinely ordained begetting. They open with the name of Zeus the King (18) but they next address an Aigina who is both nymph and city as they prepare for a scene that will take place on Olympus (21-61).

3. You* he transported to
      Oinopa's isle! He
    couched you and you gave him Aiakos,
    godlike and praised above all other men by his
    thunder-voiced father. Even among the immortals
      he served as judge and his sons,
    like theirs, lovers of war, became   25
      bravest of all in the
    service of bronze-clashing battle, yet
    temperate ever and prudent.
    All this the gathered immortals
    remembered when Zeus and splendid Poseidon
      fell into strife over
    Thetis as bride, each wanting her as his own.
    Lust ruled them both, but the
    gods in their undying wisdom let   30
      neither one enter her bed. They

55

4. heard and took note of
    heaven's decree when
Themis the Counsellor spoke, naming Thetis as
destined to bring forth a son more
powerful than his sire – the bolt in his hand
    stronger than lightning or than the tireless
trident – should she be mated with   35
    Zeus or with one of his
brothers. 'Come,' she said, 'this you must
stop! Let her lie in the bed of a mortal
that she may watch as her son dies in battle
though he be equal to Ares in
    strength, to a fire-bolt in
swiftness of foot! This is my counsel:
Give her as heaven-sent bride-prize to
Aiakid Peleus, famed as the most pious man   40
    Iolkos' plain ever nourished!

5. Send word at once
    straight to the unchanging
cavern of Chiron, for Nereus' daughter must
not for a second time bring us her
dowry of discord. Let her instead, during evenings at
    midmonth, loosen her fair virgin halter
tamed by that hero!' So she spoke,   45
    urging the children of
Kronos, and they in consent bowed their
immortal heads, nor were her words without
fruit for we're told that the two lords†
sanctioned this marriage for Thetis. For men as yet
    ignorant, poets' tongues
pictured the deeds of the youthful Achilles –

he who bloodied the vine-rich
Mysian plain as drops of black gore   50
   rained down from Telephus. He

6. bridged a return for the
     Atreids, set Helen free,
  and with his lance cut out the sinews of
  Trojans who dared for a time to resist his
  man-slaying work – Memnon, fierce in his pride,
    Hektor, and other great lords for whom Achilles,
  favouring wind of the Aiakids,   55
    opened the way to Persephone's
  palace, while he brought glory to
  Aigina and his own line. Songs, when he died,
  did not desert him for Maidens‡ of
  Helikon stood at his funeral
    pyre and his tomb to
  pour out their many-voiced threnody. It seemed
  right to the gods that a brave man, even in
  death, should be given as theme for the   60
    hymns of these goddesses.

*Aigina as nymph †Zeus and Poseidon ‡Muses

As Achilles was assigned as subject of the Muses' hymns, so a second victor from this family has been assigned to Pindar. The boxer Nikokles, cousin to Kleandros, is briefly recognised as 'one who captured the Isthmian celery crown and conquered all who lived round about with fists that none could escape!' (63-5). Then the song returns to the young man who is present, remembering lesser triumphs at Megara and Epidauros, and ending with the suggestion that Kleandros is like Achilles because, following upon threatened chaos, he too has behaved as an Aiakid and crowded his years with conspicuous action (69-70).

> Let
> one of his agemates take myrtle and
> weave for Kleandros an elegant pankratic
> crown! The contests at Megara
> gave him success, as in the past did the
>   games of the boys
> at Epidauros! The good man may readily
> give praise, for his was no quiet youth-time
> shy of bold deeds and   70
>   hidden away in a snake's lair!

Still stricken by recent losses, the boys and men who have come together in the hall of Kleandros' father have been reassured by an ode that produces a supremely positive definition of mortality. Unlike the gods, men who must die may rejoice in sons stronger than themselves, celebrating their deeds with unconstrained praise.[3]

Heredity and divine sponsorship were necessary to victory but it was finally the contender's own trained will that brought him into contest and let him endure. This truth was given its plainest mythic statement in another ode for an Aiginetan boy, Nemean 3. This time the young victor, Aristokleidas, son of a certain Aristophanes, does not display his new fame in his father's house, but with a (somewhat delayed, 80) performance at a building close to Apollo's temple, the Thearion (70), or hall of the god's Delegates, among whom the family evidently served. In spite of these sacred surroundings, however, the ode itself directly reflects the youth of its pankratic victor and is dominated throughout by the notion of progress from one status to another. It begins, indeed, by miming its own advance from poetic impulse to choral action, as the singers momentarily speak for Pindar himself, in the act of consigning his song to them (1-18):

1. Mother of singers, sovereign Muse, I beg you –
   now in the sacred Nemean month, come to this
   guest-loving Aigina, Doric Isle!
   Here beside Asopos' waters young
   craftsmen of sweetly sung revels are waiting,   5
   mad for a signal from you. Each deed has its
   separate thirst, and triumph in contest craves song,
   best comrade of courage and crowns, so

   send an abundance, drawn from my skill! You are his
   daughter – open a laud for the Ruler of Heaven while   10
   I set parts for these echoing
   voices and for the lyre! Sweet
   work will be theirs who embellish a land where
   Myrmidons dwelt, for Aristokleidas
   (aided by you*) brought no stain of dishonour to   15
   their famous ranks, when tested in savage

ep. pankratic company! He brings instead the
    victory song, poultice for pains of exhaustion
        felt on the deep Nemean plain.

*the Muse

The name of Aristokleidas causes a shift to direct praise, but this is at once interrupted by a glimpse of the exploits of Herakles, emphasised as examples of ultimate daring. These lines are playfully labelled as an enthusiastic digression (19-

29), while they establish the motif of travel over water which was a familiar emblem of initiation:

> Fair in himself, Aristophanes' boy matches his 20
> beauty with deeds and mounts to the heights of
>   valour – though no man can readily
> enter the untried sea beyond Herakles' pillars,

> 2. boundaries set by that hero-god, marking the sailor's
> uttermost stretch. He mastered proud maritime
> beasts and alone charted the shallows,
> mapped out the land, then touched at the 25
> end that fixed his return. But, o my heart, why
> beach me on this far shore? I ask you to
> carry my song to Aiakos and to his race, for
> Justice says: Praise what is noble!

Now it is Aiakos' name that marks an arrival, for the song has reached its true mythic goal, that hero's descendants, the Aiakids who are objects of special reverence for the boys and men of Aigina. Responding to their own exhortations, the singers resolve to consider these figures, and they touch on the youthful adventures of the two sons, Peleus and Telamon, as examples of strengths bred in the bone. This, however, is only preparation for their announcement of the ultimate name, that of the Aiakid grandson, Achilles (43), sounded as the cap to a wise saying about daring as a quality not to be learned (32- 63).

> Peleus, shaping his
> conquering shaft, rejoiced in old
> virtues, he who, alone and bereft of his

army, took Iolkos, then gave ocean-born   35
Thetis a fall! Fighting beside Iolaos, fierce
Telamon finished Laomedon*, then

ep. followed his friend against bronze-armed
Amazon archers, nor did fright ever
   stop him or blunt his resolve! Inborn
honour gives weight to a man, while he whose   40
ambition is learned pants after this and that, in
   blindness, his foot never sure as he
foolishly samples thousands of glorious exploits.

3. Pale-haired Achilles, a child in the care of Philyra†,
toyed with bold deeds – he twirled his small spear,
then sent it swift as the wind to   45
bloody the coats of furious lions,
or kill a boar! When he was six, he brought his
first gasping corpses back to the
Kronian centaur and, through the following
years, Athena and Artemis marvelled   50

as he took deer, not with entangling nets or with
dogs, but racing on his two feet! Mine is an
old tale – how in his troglodyte cave
deep-thinkng Chiron housed Jason,
Asklepios too, teaching the soothing practice of
pharmacy. He gave Thetis, of glorious womb, to her   55
husband and cared for her powerful son,
training his temper in fitting pursuits, that,

ep. when gusting sea-winds should take him to Troy,
he might resist the Dardanian war-cries   60
   (Phrygian, Lydian, too) and,

61

mixed in close combat with Ethiope warriors, might
hammer this purpose into his will:
   'No return home for their mightiest
lord, the furious Memnon, kin to Helenos!'

*in the first siege of Troy   †mother of Chiron

The gasping lions bear witness to the weight of an 'inborn
honour,' but Memnon, yet to be slaughtered at Troy,
measures the necessary effect of a teacher on the will of one
who is victor by nature. Valour can't be taught but the heroic
will can be trained, and the singers enforce this notion by
casting Achilles' supreme resolve in the voice of Chiron. This
is a song about learning, one that leads its auditors from the
women's quarters into the house of the initiation-master
where hunters whose blood is fearless learn to be warriors of
unbending will. And meanwhile, Aristokleidas' rough
pankratic fight has been likened to the supreme exploit of the
most glorious of Aiakid heroes, and so it is time for
thoughtful jubilation, tempered here by the presence of
Apollo's representatives in a space that belongs to that god.
Youthful courage, mature counsel, and elderly wisdom are all
present, but all must be practised with a sense of mortal limitations (74-5):

4. Light from these Aiakid deeds shines far. Yours,
    Zeus, is the blood, yours the contest tossed by this   65
    hymn to the voices of boys to be
    sung as a local joy! Shouts suit
    Aristokleidas, victor whose triumph adds
    fame to this isle and splendid concerns to the
    much honoured House of the Pythian Delegates.   70

Power shines out in mid-trial, where one is
meant for pre-eminence, be he child among children,
man among men, or in the third age. Such are the portions
we mortals have, while Fate holds four
virtues* in harness, the last being
care for the present task, and of these
not one is absent today! Farewell, my friend! I
offer this musical sip of honey and white milk,
dew-frothed and borne (a bit late) on the

ep. breath of Aiolian pipes! Wild for his distant   80
    prey, the eagle's swift claw strikes at the
       bloodied kill while chattering
    jackdaws huddle below. Now, thanks to
    Klio on high, and to your own prize-winning
       temper, light comes from Nemea,
    Megara, and Epidauros, to shine upon you!

*courage, justice, wisdom and concentration

Youth is by nature bold, maturity able to judge, while old age is wise but all these virtues must be exercised with a consciousness of the temporary and chancy quality of human life. So this chorus of boys solemnly informs the men gathered at the Thearion. For the singers the immediate task is to end a song, and following their own advice they swoop upon their friend like an eagle on his prey and leave him bathed in a glory that takes its beginning with the Aiakids.

Ajax, who fell on his own sword, would seem at first glance to be wholly inappropriate to the celebration of a boy's victory. His was a contest not won, but lost, yet Pindar chose him as the central mythic figure for Nemean 8, an ode composed for an Aiginetan boy and his father. Deinias has taken a crown in the boys' double-stade race at Nemea, and Megas (now dead) had long ago won in the same race, apparently without being adequately celebrated, so the present song serves both. The boy, at the time of his victory, had just reached adolescence and the singers begin with a call to the goddess of ripe youth, an invocation that carries a whiff of eroticism (1-8).

1. Hora, mistress of love's holy sweets,
      Kyprian herald en-
    throned upon eyelids of boys and girls, one
    suitor you raise up with gentle hands, another you
          treat in an opposite fashion!
    Best pleasure comes when a timely choice,
    made among braver desires, takes its prize.   5

    Such loves, bringers of Kypris' best gifts,
        served at the couch where
    Zeus lay with Aigina, whence came a son*,
    king of Oinona and best in counsel and might!

    *Aiakos

Hora brought a nubile nymph to Zeus and so determined the foundation of Aigina-Oinona, the city of the victor and his father, but this emphasis on youthful sexuality is dramatically abandoned as the chorus announces a mythic novelty, then depicts a notorious suicide. They summon a vision of Ajax, who destroyed himself when the Achaeans denied him the golden arms of Achilles and gave them to Odysseus instead (19-34).

Light feet at a standstill, I take breath, then speak!
Tales are re-told, but a new-found invention,   20
    put to the test, is at risk.
Fame is a feast for the envious, who
turn from the lesser to seize on what's fine.

Such envy bit into Telamon's son*,
    thrusting him onto his
sword. Bold at heart, the man of no words
loses his match with oblivion, while a   25
    slippery lie takes the prize!
Secret Greek ballots favoured Odysseus, but
Ajax, the gold armour lost, wrestled with gore.

ep. Unequal too were the wounds cut in warm
    enemy flesh as, hard-pressed, their two spears
    sheltered the new-killed corpse of Achilles, or   30
        afterwards laboured through
    days of destruction! Yes, loathsome slander is
    ancient, the ally of ugly suggestions,
    scheming and ever inventing injurious
        taunts. It violates
    brilliance but fosters a decadent fame where
        no worthy deeds can be shown.

*Ajax

What has this glimpse of an Ajax fallen on his own sword
done for the praise of two island runners who both took crowns
at Nemea? The episode is introduced as a bit of rhetoric, an
example that demonstrates the power of envy, and the hero
remains a mere representative phantom until the final lines of

his stanza (26-7). There he is at last named, and there the listener's senses are for the first time engaged by concrete images – of secret ballots, gold armour, and the blood with which Ajax paradoxically 'wrestles'. These point to a tale in which the armour of Achilles was granted to Odysseus, not by vocal Greek chieftains, and not by Trojan captives, but by the Achaean host, led astray by the clever man's slanderous eloquence. These ballots, however (emphasised at the opening of line 26), impose the concept of enumeration, and this prepares for a dramatic reversal that takes place in the pause between stanza and epode.

Unequal votes cast for Odysseus and Ajax brought the unequal rewards of golden armour and a pool of gore, but the services repaid in this way were likewise unequal, in an opposite sense ('Unequal too ...', 28ff.). With the blood of Ajax still in his mind's eye, the spectator has been sent backwards in time and onto the battlefield, where the corpse of Achilles is being defended from Trojan outrage. There he is to count, not ballots, but 'wounds cut in warm enemy flesh' (28-9) by the two rivals, and the result of his tally has been fixed since Homer's time. The numbers for Ajax are overwhelming and so, as the song momentarily brings that hero back to violent life, the audience, by making its tally, rights the wrong that was done him. The force that destroyed Ajax was 'loathsome slander ... the ally of ugly suggestions, scheming, and ever inventing injurious taunts' (31-3), but the present performance restores him with its praise, and this leads to a general resolution which, in turn, finally produces a restoration of praise for Megas (35-51).

3. O father Zeus, let this never be
     my chosen mode! I would
    take simpler paths and leave, when I die, no bad

fame to my sons. Some pray for gold, others for
    land, but I'd wrap these limbs in clay,
favoured by townsmen for praising the
praiseworthy, blaming the doers of wrong!

Excellence grows like the trunk of a tree   40
    under fresh dew; it is
raised to the sky's liquid heights by men who love
justice and song. Friends fill various needs,
    best where trouble is, but joy
too seeks a pledge from an eye that is
faithful. O Megas, to bring back your life – this

ep. I cannot do (that were an empty hope), but for the   45
    Chariads* and for your homeland it's easy to
raise up a Muse-stone marking the duplicate
    triumphs of two pairs of
feet! I rejoice as I shout out the boast earned by your
deed, for with magical chants one may deaden the
pain of hard toil. Truly, the victory   50
    hymn and its revel were
born long ago, even before the
    strife of Adrastos with Kadmos' sons†.

*the tribe of Megas   †when the Nemean Games were founded

The boys who sang Nemean 8 reminded themselves and
their elders that, beyond the exaltation of the victory moment,
beyond even the joy of seeing a son gain a victory, there was
another form of good fortune that all might hope for – an
unstained reputation. Anyone could strive for good fame, and
all were bound to bring the fair deeds of others to light – to be,

in other words, the reverse of Odysseus. Pindar has supplied the whole company with a kind of oath of adulthood – a promise to maintain the constant self-scrutiny of praise and blame that is essential to any community.

3

Celebrations for Men

Pythian 9; Olympian 9; Olympian 7; Isthmian 1; Olympian 6

In the early fifth century BC hundreds of well-to-do Greek men set out every year to test themselves in one or more of the competitions held at Olympia, Delphi, Isthmia or Nemea. For a man in his 20s or 30s, of good family and with some athletic aptitude, participation in the crown games was a duty owed to his ancestors, his descendants, and to his city. What is more, athletic success brought an eminence that could attract an advantageous marriage or launch a man in politics. And finally there were contacts to be made with men from other parts of the Hellenic world – Asia Minor, North Africa, the Aegean islands, Sicily and South Italy. One might even meet a wise philosopher or a famous poet among the crowd of spectators.

The games at Olympia, traditionally founded by Herakles, honoured Zeus and came every four years, at the second full moon after the solstice (late July or early August), at which time a general truce was proclaimed all over mainland Greece (note the 'truce-bearing messengers' of Isthmian 2.23). Contestants spent a preliminary month in training at Elis, then, at the opening of the festival, they entered the sanctuary to be examined: they had to be Greek, could not be guilty of murder or sacrilege, and were required to swear to abide by all rules. On the next morning the games began with equestrian events in the hippodrome – horse race, mule-cart race, and chariot race. In the afternoon all moved to the stadium for the pentathlon, with its sequential competitions in running, jumping, discus throw, and javelin cast, the various winners being finally paired in wrestling matches to determine the ultimate champion. On the following day there were processions, the slaughter of a hundred oxen for Zeus, and a great banquet from which all went off to watch the boys' competitions. On the last day of competition came the running events: stadium (200 metres), double stadium, and long distance (at Olympia 24 stades, or about three miles). These were followed by the fierce two-man matches between boxers, wrestlers and pankratists, the pairs determined by lot. Last of all was the *hoplitodromos*, a footrace in which contestants wearing helmets and greaves and carrying heavy shields ran 400 metres.

Throughout the festival each event closed with the herald's announcement of a victor's name, patronymic and city, and with the presentation of a woolly headband, or *tainia*, which the winner placed on his own head. At night these successful men and their supporters would gather in the moonlight for impromptu fire-lit revels as 'the whole precinct filled with festive joy' (Olympian 10.76-7). Then, on the fifth day, all who had attended the festival watched as the judges distributed crowns made of wild olive cut with a golden sickle. The happy victors were pelted with leaves and flowers and, ready now to 'draw the deep breath that comes after toil' (Olympian 8.7), they went off to a ceremonial dinner. On the morrow they would depart, carrying the wreaths that would provoke further recognition and praise when they reached home.

The other three festivals showed local differences but followed much the same schedule. The games at Delphi were held in the third year of each Olympiad, in August, in honour of long-haired Apollo, father of the healer, Asklepios, and god of bow and lyre. Only here were there contests for musicians as well as for athletes (Pythian 12 celebrates the crowning of a pipe player come from Sicily). The contest grounds were in an area called Kirrha just below the temple, victory was signalled by a wreath of bay leaves, and the games were called Pythian because the oracular shrine on the southern slope of Parnassos stood where Apollo had slain the first lord of the place, a monster named Pytho. Delphi was notorious for its equestrian events – six of Pindar's twelve Pythian odes celebrate chariot victories – but all the traditional contests were held, boys' competitions alternating with those of men. At Isthmia, near Corinth, games traditionally founded in 582 BC were held close to the temple of Poseidon, the sea-god who shared this holy place with a pre-Olympian hero, Melikertes, pulled up from the sea and honoured with a funerary cult (Pausanias 1.44.7ff.). Held every two years in late springtime (April/May), and offering a crown of dry parsley, these were in the fifth century the most frequented of the four crown contests (though, in open rivalry with Olympia, men from Elis were not allowed to compete). And alternating with the Isthmian games, but in July, a festival took place at Nemea at the sanctuary of Zeus in remembrance of Herakles' victory when wrestling with the Nemean lion. As at Isthmia, there was a local hero, the infant Opheltes/Archemoros, whose funeral games were celebrated in this place by the seven legendary leaders of the Argive army when on their way to attack Thebes. The Nemean crown was of fresh parsley.

In the men's gymnastic events, whatever the festival, stature and weight were as decisive as skill and determination and a certain brutality was essential. (Vase-painters depicted athletes as creatures with small heads but enormous shoulders and buttocks.) Boxing was made bloody with leather-bound fists, and the contest continued with no break until one man was unconscious or had signalled surrender.[1] Wrestlers were forbidden to bite or gouge, but were allowed to bend (but not break) one another's fingers, as well as to trip and kick, and the prize went to the one who three times forced his opponent's knees to the ground. In the pankration, contestants might legally throttle or strangle, punch, kick or slap, and biting and gouging of eyes, though technically prohibited, often occurred. It was permissible to jump on a fallen opponent, and the fight ended only when one man was unconscious or incapacitated. Even the non-confrontational trials reflected the regulation of an essential aggressiveness, as was explicit in the heavy-armed race with its combination of the trappings of war with an action that was formally restricted. In all these events, raw violence was tempered and focussed, as if to exemplify an original shift from anarchy to the first forms of civilisation, and this became a frequent motif in the odes that Pindar made for victors necessarily endowed with a fearsome strength.

Festival contest was considered a symbolic substitute for earthly disorder and Herakles made this plain when, after his destructive revenge upon Augeas, he used the 'best gifts of war' in his foundation of the Olympic games (Olympian 10.43-9, above, p. 19). To use force according to strict terms was a public gesture towards Hellenic self-discipline, as Pindar made plain in Pythian 9, a light-hearted ode that celebrated a certain Telesikrates, 'shield-bearing Pythian victor' whose city was Cyrene (Kyrana). This man had taken his crown in the heavy-armed race and, as a parallel to the mortal battle-spirit that submits to contest rules, the song proposes a divine lust that submits to the customs of marriage. It tells of a smitten Apollo, tempted to take a nymph by open violence, but persuaded instead to play by the rules of gods and men, with telling results: supreme divine pleasure, of course, but also the transformation of a wild girl into a powerful queen, the foundation of a luxurious city in Africa, and the birth of Aristaios, patron divinity of domesticated animals. The nymph is Kyrana, daughter of Hypseos, a violent Lapith, a 'maid yet untamed' who chooses to live like a boy on the slopes of Mount Pelion (16-70).

> Hypseos nourished the
> fair-armed Kyrana in childhood, but she
>   cared not at all for the journeying shuttle
> nor for stay-at-home suppers with friends.
> Rather, with spear or the blade of a sword, she would   20
> challenge wild beasts and
> slaughter them, bringing much
> safety and peace to her father's herds.
>   Scant time she spent with that
> sweet bedmate, sleep, as it
> settled, towards dawn, on her eyelids!   25

> 2. Once, as she fought with a furious lion, un-
> armed and alone, Apollo the Far-shooter
> chanced to see. He shouted to Chiron:
> 'Son of Philyra! Come from your hallowed cave and
> marvel with me at the courage and   30
>   strength of this girl – see how she
> keeps a cool head as she fights,
> heart in command of her work,
> wits not frozen by fear!
> What mortal parent has she? From whose
>   house was she taken, to
> dwell in these shadowy mountains, testing her

unrestrained boldness? Might I stretch out a   35
glorious hand to pluck some sweet-scented
grass from her couch?' The spirited Centaur gave a quick
smile, raised an eyebrow, and spoke:
　　'Phoibos, the keys to all sacred
loves are wisely kept secret by
Peitho*. This is forbidden by
shame, among gods, as among   40
men – to enter a sweet virgin
　　bed in broad daylight!

ep. Surely soft passion has twisted your speech, for
　　you, by decree, cannot touch an untruth.
　　　　Would you, my lord, ask the girl's
　　ancestors – you who know the sure end of all
　　things, and the way? You can number the leaves that   45
　　burgeon in spring, the
　　sand-grains that move in
　　river or sea, driven by waves and wind!
　　　　You know all that will come and
　　whence! But, if I'm to be
　　matched with Wisdom itself, I'll   50

3.　speak! You are come to this vale as her
　　spouse; you will carry her over the sea to a
　　wondrous garden belonging to Zeus where, gathering
　　men from an island to settle a plain-bound hill, you will
　　give her the rule of a city. On   55
　　　　this very day, Libya, lady of
　　broad fields, will joyfully welcome her
　　into a palace of gold, as your
　　bride. A portion of earth will be

lawfully hers, nor will it lack in
    beasts or fruit-bearing trees.

She will give birth to a son whom Hermes will
take from his mother and carry aloft to   60
Ge and the Hours, seated on high, and they, with the
babe on their knees, will drip nectar into his
mouth, and ambrosia, making him deathless, like
    Zeus or Apollo! Watcher of herds,
dear to his fellows, for some his
name will be Ruler of Forest and
Flocks, Aristaios for others!'   65
Thus he urged the god on towards an
    ultimate marital joy.

ep. Action is swift, the road short, when a
    god is in haste. That day sufficed: they met and were
        joined in Libya's gold-furnished
    chamber, here in this city now hers –
    fairest of all and known for its contests!   70

*Persuasion

Chiron's words promise the creation of a friendly demigod,
Aristaios, companion of hunters and herdsmen, while more
immediately they transform a potential act of rape into the
formally sanctioned marriage that was announced by the
opening lines of the song. There, in a quick preview of their
mythic scene, the dancers had spoken of their city, Kyrana, as
the place where Apollo, having 'ravished a maid yet untamed
from Pelion's echoing valleys,' finally set the girl down, to be
greeted by Aphrodite and given her formal sanction (9-12).

Silver-shod Kypris welcomed her Delian
visitor, touching his god-made chariot
lightly and sprinkling his sweet marriage bed with
reverent awe as she yoked them in wedlock ...

Marriage that regulates lust is analogous to the festival
contest that regulates aggression, and at the ode's end this
ruling notion is made explicit in a quick tale about
Alexidamos, one of the victor's ancestors, a Greek settler who
won his local bride in a footrace. The girl was just come of age,
the beautiful daughter of a Libyan noble, and she had many
suitors (109-25).

All wished to pluck gold-crowned Hebe's ripe
fruit but her father, who wanted a glorious   110
wedding, thought on Danaos – how in
long-ago Argos he had arranged the swiftest of
nuptials for forty-eight daughters, all before
   noon! Marking a course, he had
placed the whole girlish troupe at its finish,
announcing that swiftness of
foot should decide which of the   115
would-be husbands might take
   which of the maids as his bride.

ep. This too was the way of the Libyan father in
   choosing a groom for his girl. He dressed her and
     set her as prize at the end of a
   course, to be taken by him who, racing ahead,
   first touched her robe. And it was   120
   Alexidamos, leading a swift field, who
   took the fair maid by her hand, to

draw her away through crowds of nomads.
Many the leaves and
garlands they tossed – many the
victory plumes he had already taken! 125

The war-like spirit of Telesikrates has submitted to Delphic rules, as Apollo's lust did to heaven's regulations, and there is a strong suggestion that his victory will be rewarded by marriage, as was that of his ancestor, Alexidamos. A somewhat more serious note is struck in Olympian 9, made for Epharmostos, a young but widely successful wrestler from Eastern Lokris, just beneath Parnassos, where the lesser Ajax received special honours. Surprisingly, neither father nor tribe is named for this victor, but instead the song claims Titans, Zeus, and the Stone People as his forebears, for its predominant motif is the mixing of divine and autochthonous elements in the first communities to be formed after the Flood.[2]

Opuntian Lokris, where the celebration is held, is praised as a 'city allotted to Themis and saviour Eunomia, her child' (15-16) – that is, as a place that knows settled order and the rule of law – but this condition, like the joys of victory and music, comes only 'as some divine power decrees' (29). Indeed, when it emerged from the flood-waters this spot of land was, like the whole earth, barren of mankind, and even with the coming of Deukalion and Pyrrha, the only flood-survivors, its population was not fixed. Those two descendants of Titans produced their own offspring, while they also planted stones that became people (there is a pun between *laes,* stones, and *laoi,* people), but the race of the Opuntians came into being only when their grand-daughter, Protogeneia, was impregnated by Zeus and brought her unborn son – a gift from that god – to a childless king named Lokros who ruled among Stone People. Grown to manhood, the hero-prince, Opous, gathered friends around him, among them the father of Patroklos, and so Opuntian Lokris became not only a place of god-sponsored order but also of masculine fellowship, as embodied in Achilles and his favourite companion. Today's victor, then, as he brings a Zeus-given crown from Olympia to this same city, reflects and confirms Protogeneia's founding gift. What is more, he also, like Opous, represents friendship, for he shares today's celebration with his guest-friend, Lampromachos. This pair, on one day, had together taken two Isthmian crowns (84-5).

As companions of Epharmostos, the singers promise to be more musical than the troupe that shouted with him on the night of his victory (1-10, see above, p. 17). Then, after praising the orderly 'city of shining trees' (15-20) and skirting the notion that strife could occur among divinities (30-5), the dancers remind themselves that 'casting the gods in scandalous roles is a hateful skill' (36-7). Their subject is Lokris and the creation of civic harmony from chaos, battle and contest, and so they begin with the flood's two survivors and continue with the development of a new mortal race that is in part divine, in part born of the earth (40-79).

> ... Leave war and violence
> far from the gods as your tongue now
> touches the city of Protogeneia!
> Settling there, by order of thundering Zeus,
> Deukalion and Pyrrha, with no act of love,
> founded a race made of pebbles called   45
> People of Stone. Open a pathway of
> verses for them – praise old wine, but
> songs of a more recent vintage!

ep. Men still tell of a watery deluge that
    swallowed the black earth, and of the sudden   50
    ebb-tide that followed by
    Zeus' contrivance. From Deukalion and
    Pyrrha your ancestors came,
        armed youths descended from
    daughters of Iapetos' race and from   55
    Kronos' magnificent sons.
        They ruled as native-born kings

3. until the lord of Olympus
    snatched up the daughter of
        Opous from Elis,
    couched her in secret on Mainolos' slopes*, then
    brought her to Lokros, lest that man should   60
    end his days childless. She held holiest seed and the
    king looked with joy on the son he was
    given, naming him after the mother's sire†,
    that he might be, as a man,
    wondrous in form and in deeds, and he gave him the   65
    People of Stone and the rule of their city.

    Friends came from Pisa and Thebes,
    Arkadia and Argos, to
        join him but he
    honoured Menoitios most of all, child of
    Aktor and Aigina, whose son‡   70
    went with the Atreid host to the Mysian plain to
    stand with Achilles, he alone, when
    Telephos routed the valorous Greeks and
    threatened their beached ships –
    proof, to a sensible man, of the fierce   75
    will of Patroklos! That was when Thetis' son

79

ep. ordered him never to stand at a distance when
   furious Ares was near, but to stay
   close to his own man-killing spear.
   Let me be lifted away in the Muses'   80
   car as I search for words – let
       daring and skill follow
   me! Because of his valour and status as
   guest-friend, I come to honour the
       Isthmian crown of Lampromachos,

4. won on a day when the two men were   85
   victors! ...

   *in Arkadia
   †Opous
   ‡Patroklos

A catalogue of Epharmostos' many past victories follows,
one of them taken at Marathon where, barred from the beardless class, he had wrestled with men without being thrown.
Now he brings the supreme prize to Lokris and to its hero,
Ajax, and with their last words the dancers exhort themselves
to give him the praise his record demands (101-end).

   Everywhere, what comes by nature is strongest.
   Many seek fame with skills they have learned but
   actions achieved in the absence of god
   suffer no damage when greeted with silence.

ep. Some roads lead further than others, nor does a   105
   single ambition nourish us all.
   Steep is the path of the arts

but as you offer this prize, be bold –
shout it straight out, that this man was
   born, by god's will,
ready of hand, limbs able, eyes brave.   110
Now, o Ajax*, at your feast he
places a crown on your altar!

  *the lesser Ajax, son of Oileus

   Praise for a mature victor already known throughout Greece
called for a different approach. Olympian 7 was made for
Diagoras of Rhodes, the son of a victor, the father of victors to
come, and a boxer who had been triumphant at Isthmia, Nemea
and Delphi. In these circumstances envy from men, even from
gods, was to be expected and Pindar ingeniously responded with
a long and complex song that described a world of mortal error
and weakness, shaped by the interference of divinities who offer
a restorative tolerance even where it is not deserved.

   In this ode for a gigantic Rhodian boxer, three distorted
actions are depicted – an imperfect divine apportionment, a
botched sacrifice, and a revenge that shed kin blood – while
the account itself is made disorderly by a reversal of their
chronological order. Nevertheless, all this bungling culminates
in the foundation of what will become present-day Rhodes,
the establishment of the games that will train up the victorious
Diagoras, and a performance that confirms the poet as master
of the epinician genre. (This is the ode that was set up in letters
of gold in the temple of Athena at Lindos.) With their first
words the singers strike a note of intimate hilarity, greeting the
fortunate victor as a father might greet a new son-in-law, but
from the beginning they also sing of Rhodes, its cities, and all
its inhabitants (1-19).

1. As, with a lavish hand a man takes a cup
   foaming with wine, sips, and offers it,
   wealth's golden summit,
   to a young son-in-law, hearth to
        hearth – adding grace to the banquet
   and paying honour to his new kin,   5
        making him envied among gathered
   friends for a marriage of like with like – so

   I offer nectar, sweet fruit of the mind and
   gift of the Muses, to men who take
   prizes at Pytho
   or at Olympia! Blessed is   10
        he whom fair report seizes.
   Charis, the gracious giver of bloom,
        looks upon one, then another, as
   musical strings join the babbling pipe.

ep. Now as I come with Diagoras,
        both sounds are heard! I sing of Rhodes,
   born from the sea, daughter of
        Kypris and Helios' bride,
   that I may praise this giant contender,   15
        paying the wages of one
   crowned for his boxing at Delphi and at the
   Alpheos*! I shall sing too of his
        sire, Damagetos, beloved of Justice – both
   dwell in the isle of three cities†, near Asia's coast, with
   spearmen from Argos as neighbours.

   *at Olympia   †Rhodes

3. Celebrations for Men

As the song continues both family and city are pictured as marked by violence and disorderly confusion. The singers name Herakles as founder of the victor's line, thus suggesting an original glory, but then, using an ominous proverb as a bridge, they move at once to that hero's son, Tlepolemos. It was his murder of his own great-uncle that caused his exile from Tiryns and so made him the founder of Rhodes (24-34).

> Errors hang numberless over men's
> minds and none knows the fate that is   25
>
> best for a man to encounter – now, or in the end. At
> Tiryns, a man took his olive-wood
> sceptre to murder a
> kinsman, Likymnios, one who had
>   come from Midea – and that angry
> man was Tlepolemos, this island's founder!   30
>   Storms trouble even the minds of the
> wise. He consulted the golden-haired god*

> ep. who, from his incense-filled cell,
>   counselled a voyage
> out from the rough cliffs of Lerna and
>   over to this sea-girt land where the
> king of the gods had long ago buried a
>   city in deep golden snow ...

*Apollo

Though it comes first in the song, this tale of settlement from Tiryns is the latest of the legendary events that will be related. Apollo's oracular response has identified Rhodes with

a particular miracle, and this draws the singers back to an event
that occurred long before the time of Herakles and
Tlepolemos. The fabled 'golden snow' had come (33-53)

...

after Athena had leapt from the peak of   35
her father's brow, thanks to Hephaistos'
    skill with his axe, her echoing battle-cry
causing the heavens to shudder while Ge, the earth's
mother, shuddered as well!

3. Helios, light-giving child of Hyperion,
   then set a task for his sons to fulfil: 40
   they should be first to
   set up a high-built shrine for the
      new goddess, there to gladden both
   father and spear-wielding maid* with
      holiest victims. Awe, born of forethought,
   brings men both courage and joy, yet a strange

   cloud of forgetting may settle upon them to   45
   hide the straight path from their minds. So these
   islanders went up,
   carrying no seed of flame! Their
      citadel precinct was founded with
   rites that lacked fire, yet Zeus nonetheless
      brought a pale cloud that rained
   copious gold down upon them, and the   50

ep. grey-eyed goddess herself gave to their
      hands supreme skill in all
   crafts; soon statues like animate
      creatures stood in their streets,

making them famous. Where men are wise, art
   wrought without guile has
greater effect ...

*Zeus and Athena

At this point the victor's homeland has been identified, not
just as an Apolline reward for a kin-crime, but also as a place
where failure to fulfil a god's command brought riches, artistic
skill, and fame. (Hidden in the praise of Rhodian art as free from
deceit, there is probably a negative reference to the legendary
Telchines, an original population of sinister craftsmen-wizards
who were replaced by descendants of Helios.) The description,
however, is not yet complete and as they continue the singers
drop back to their deepest point in mythic time to tell how the
island itself came to belong to Helios only through his own
tardiness in arriving at a meeting of the gods (54-76).

                  Stories from
long ago tell that when Zeus shared out the
    earth with the other immortals, Rhodes was not   55
seen on the broad sea's surface, but rested still,
hidden away in those salt depths, nor was

4. Helios present. No lot fell to him, no least
    portion of earth, though he was a
    sacred divinity!   60
Zeus, once reminded, offered a fresh
    cast, but the other refused – he had
seen, growing up from the floor of the grey
    sea, a land fruitful for men and
promising kindly pasture for sheep.

He begged Lachesis*, the gold-crowned, to lift up her
hands and, true to the gods' solemn oath, to   65
join Kronos' son in
granting this island – once risen and
     visible in the bright
air – to him, to be his for all time. And the
     thrust of his words became truth, for this
island did rise from the liquid sea to be

ep. held now by Helios, father of   70
     sharp shafts of light and
master of fire-breathing steeds! With
     Rhodos† as bride, he sired seven sons,
their minds far wiser than those of the
     children of men. One of these
fathered three brothers, Kamiros,
Lindos and – eldest – Ialysos, princes who
     shared their inherited land,
making three portions, each taking several cities,   75
his own seat called by his name.

*one of the Fates   †the local nymph

Such was the island that Tlepolemos found when he followed
the Delphic command, and the singers now return to him and
to the immediate occasion (77-end).

5. There sweet ransom from bitter misfortune
     came to Tlepolemos, founder from
Tiryns, as if for a
god – sheep in procession, moving towards   80
     sacrifice, and too a judging of athletic

contests that twice gave Diagoras crowns.
    Four times at Isthmia he took the
prize; at Nemea twice, and on Athens' heights.

Known to the bronze at Argos and to the tripods of
Thebes and Arkadia, he won in the
    games of Boiotia,   85
and at Pellana, too. Six times a
    victor at Aigina, and a like
record is wrought in Megarian stone! O father
    Zeus, Atabyrion's* lord, honour the
hymn ordained for Olympic victors, and

ep. honour this man who invented the
    virtue of fists!
    Grant him reverent thanks from   90
    strangers and townsmen for, taught by the
upright minds of his forebears, he follows the
    path that hates arrogance.
Do not obscure the seed they have
shared since the epoch of Kallianax†! When
    Eratid men celebrate triumphs, the
city holds festival too, though winds as they
change in one moment blow this way and that.   95

*mountain on Rhodes   †an ancestor

In the course of Olympian 7 the listener is drawn back to
the beginning of time and down to the bottom of the sea.
From his dining couch he watches as Rhodes rises from the
depths, having first witnessed a kin-killing, then an act of careless sacrilege, but also a golden miracle that testifies to the

divine favour that has let a magnificent athlete appear from such chaos. Treated in this way, Diagoras' victory in the boxing ring becomes the consummate expression of a fated but casual shift from stubborn disorder to regular Hellenic custom.

When, however, the crown to be celebrated was taken in one of the increasingly popular equestrian contests, the civilising aspect of victory no longer dominated Pindar's songs. Races for single mounts, for the mule-cart with its seated driver and team of two, and for chariots drawn by four horses (introduced at Olympia in 680 BC) were held at all the four crown contests and provided their most sensational moments. Lives were risked and crowds went mad, but there were two ways in which these magnificent events were less meaningful than the trials that were exclusively human. First, they were open only to the very rich, and secondly they brought glory, not to disciplined athletes who invested muscle, skill, and resolve, but to ambitious owners who risked only reputation and property. A horse was raced without saddle or stirrups, and ridden by a jockey who was the lightest and most skilled boy to be found. He might be from the owner's family, but more often he was a hired servant or a slave. And the heavily decorated chariots with their blooded teams were driven by men distinguished only for strong hands and coolness in the fearsome collisions that were part of a day's work. Chariot drivers, more than any other contestants, risked their lives as well as their bones – at Pythian 5.49, Pindar mentions a race in which forty charioteers fell – but unless they were relatives or friends of the owner they did their work for pay rather than for honour. (The Nikomachos of Isthmian 2.22 seems to have been a major exception; he drove for the royal house at Akragas, but was of high enough social status to have entertained the emissaries of the Olympic truce when they came from Elis.) And of course, whether for saddle or chariot, horses were usually trained with cruelty. In sum, then, the jockey or driver enforced an order anything but civil upon creatures unlike himself, while he displayed, not his own disciplined power, but that of animals who were someone else's purchased property. The crown, in these contests, went almost always to a man who had not himself been tried, often to one no longer young who had neither training nor skill – indeed, at the end of the century a sister of the Spartan king won at Olympia with a show of 'riches, rather than manliness', according to Xenophon (*Agesilaos* 9.6, cf. Pausanias 3.15.1). The chariot victor had only to be wealthy, fortunate, and able to bring others into his service.

These truths were necessarily reflected in the men who took part in equestrian events and in the songs which celebrated their victories. To begin with, each contender exercised a power that was potentially if not actually political, since he had to organise the bringing of extra horses or mules, trainers, stable-help, and mechanics, as well as jockeys or drivers, to the place of contest. (It may have been the family's Olympic chariot victories that demanded the disclaimer of tyrannical ambitions that comes surprisingly in a song made for a Theban boy victor: 'Finding that men of mid-rank prosper best in a city, I fault the tyrant's lot and aim at the common good – this defeats Envy!' Pythian 11.51-4.)[3] For an ambitious man, such a show of authority was desirable but dangerous, since the splendour of horse-trappings and carved and gilded chariots necessarily aroused envy, even without victory. And if he won, the victor's position was at best ambivalent since, while lesser men might almost worship, those in power could feel threatened by such blinding glory. The field athlete's condition of being peer amongst peers did not apply to a man so conspicuous, and as if in compensation – among Pindar's patrons, at any rate – non-rulers usually chose to celebrate their winning horses, mule-carts, and chariots with a certain reserve.

Perhaps a chariot victory in itself spread more than enough glory, or perhaps it was thought presumptuous for anyone but a ruler to be lavish in a his proclamation of a success so magnificent. Certainly Megakles of Athens, already banished from the city, commanded the briefest of songs and Pindar responded with a single rather constrained triad that did not mention either team or chariot, though the singers did say, as they fell silent, 'I grieve to see Envy respond to fair deeds, but even where happiness blooms and abides, it brings, so they say, both bad and good' (Pythian 7.17-21). The only full-scale ode for the chariot victory of an ordinary citizen is Isthmian 1, made perhaps around 458 BC for a young Theban whose pro-Persian family had recently returned from exile. Herodotos is the victor of the day but nonetheless there is loud praise here, not for him but instead for two mythic counterparts, Kastor and Iolaos (16-21).

> Those two,
>> bravest of heroes, one born in Thebes, one in
>>> Lakedaimon, though prime

2. chariot men, tried games of all sorts and took
    tripods, vases, and wine cups of gold to
    furbish their halls – such was their taste for   20
    victory garlands!

The success of Herodotos, by contrast, does not become a subject for boasts; indeed a similar list of his exploits is rejected – 'But to recount all of the gifts made to Herodotus and to his team by games-master, Hermes – for this my hymn is too short!' (60-3). Instead, his Isthmian chariot victory is presented only as an indication that his father's fortunes have shifted from shipwreck to survival (35-40):

> Ancestral fields at Orchomenos gave welcome when   35
> shipwreck and freezing misfortune
> cast him* ashore, badly battered, out of the
> measureless sea.
> Now the fixed fate of his fathers
> sets him again on a fair-weather course!

> *the father

The son's magnificent success will be no threat to the community because of an essential fact that the chorus has established almost as soon as they began to sing. This young man, like a true athlete, is a 'chariot-driver who does not abandon the reins to another' (15). Herodotos drove his own team, to win like an athlete, not like a ruler; he displays his fortune and his full strength for the good of the community and his song can thus end with a prayer for even more splendid crowns (64-end).

> Lifted on bright wings lent by Pierian Muses,
> may he yet garland his hand in choice   65
>   wreaths from Pytho and Elis*,
> fixing the fame of Seven-Gate Thebes! One who hides
> riches indoors, while sneering at others,
> fails to consider the soul he will render,
>   naked of glory, to Hades.

> *Delphi and Olympia

Since mules were not as fast as horses, their carts not as showy as the chariot, the mule-cart competition was the safest, both physically and politically, of all the equestrian contests. A victory taken in this more modest event could presumably be celebrated with confidence, but still a certain Psaumis, a middle-aged man of Kamarina, on the south coast of Sicily, chose to commemorate his 'tireless mules' with two very short songs (Olympians 4 and 5), rather than a full-scale performance. There is, however, one ode made on a grand scale for a victory with a mule-cart – Olympian 6, commissioned by Hagesias of Syracuse.

This victor belonged to the inner circle that supported the tyrant, Hieron, but his mother's family was rooted in Arkadia, and he evidently requested a song suitable for double performance. A certain Aineas, a member of the mainland family, received the ode from the poet (90) and trained dancers for a celebration at Stymphalos, the family seat on the southern slope of Mount Kyllene, which would then be repeated in Hieron's Syracuse. The entertainment thus had to please two very different audiences – one a group of mainland kinsmen, presumably sympathetic, the other the possibly envious court of a Sicilian ruler – but with his Olympian 6 Pindar found a safe yet splendid way to bring delight to both. His strategy was to praise the victor and his family, not for athletic, military or civic exploits, but instead for inherited prophetic powers that carried no threat, and this intention is made plain at once. The singers announce that they must work on a grand scale, since their song celebrates one who is Olympic victor, a servant at Zeus' mantic altar at Olympia, and a member of an old Syracusan family (4-6). Then, in support of his second, sacred identity, they liken Hagesias to Amphiaraos, the legendary seer rescued by Zeus and established in his own oracular shrine when the Argives retreated from Thebes (1-21).

3. Celebrations for Men

1. Pillars of gold we shall raise,
    as for the well-built porch of a
splendid abode, for our song,
at its beginning, needs a façade that
shines from afar! If a man be Olympian victor,
    guardian at Pisa of
Zeus' oracular shrine, and one of the founders of   5
famed Syracuse, what praise can he
    hope to escape as he
moves among townsmen not
    stingy with much-desired song?

Let Sostratos' son* understand – his
    foot fills this shoe! Fine deeds
done without risk, whether on
land or at sea, go without honour but, when   10
toil brings an end to a high task, many
    remember. Hagesias,
your praise is ready, the same that fell from the
tongue of Adrastos for Amphiaraos,
    Oikleës' mantic son,
as, with his shining team, earth
    seized and engulfed him!

ep. When seven pyres had consumed their dead,   15
    these words were spoken at
Thebes by Talaos' son†: 'I long for the
    eye of my army, best
prophet and best at wielding a spear!'
    Our Syracusan master of revels‡
is such a man! I am no I lover of strife,
nor am I victory-mad, but with a great

93

oath I bear witness to this, and   20
honey-voiced Muses
    lend their support!

*Hagesias †Adrastos ‡Hagesias

   Ready now to turn from the victor to his prophetic family, the singers mount an imaginary mule-cart and move into the realm of Arkadian legend. As analogue to the victor, Amphiaraos is to be replaced with a maternal ancestor, the prophet Iamos, grandson of Poseidon and son of Apollo but established at Olympia at the altar of Zeus. To discover him, the song takes a musical journey that first follows the Lakonian river, Eurotas, to find the nymph who was Iamos' grandmother, then follows his mother, Evadne, into Arkadia for his engendering and birth (22-76).

2. Come, Phintis*, yoke up your strong
     mules – do it quickly – that we may
  settle our cart on a clean
  path, to arrive at the root of this family!
  Your team knows, better than all, how to travel this   25
     road, having taken
  Olympic crowns! Hymn-gates must open for
  us, for today we will follow the
     river Eurotas to
  come in good time to the
     ford that bears Pitana's† name.

  She, so men say, couched by the
     Kronian Poseidon, bore that god's
  child, the dark-haired Evadne.   30
  Unwed, she‡ hid her burden and, when the

month came, ordered her servants to give the babe
   over to Eilatos'
son§, who dwelt in Phaisana on Alpheos' banks
ruling Arkadians. And it was
   there that Evadne first
touched Aphrodite's sweet 35
   gifts, with Apollo as guide.

ep. Not long could she hide the god's seed from the
   eye of her guardian, and
Aipytos set off for Pytho, his heart's
   anger made dumb by a
sharper concern, to ask the god's
   word on a pain past endurance.
Soon the girl loosened her red sash, set down her
silver urn under a hedge, and gave 40
birth to a god-inspired boy, while to attend her
Apollo sent Fates and
   mild Eleithyia**.

3. Iamos came from her womb and
   into the light with a sweet pang.
Weeping, she left him there on the
ground but by god's will two green-eyed snakes
nursed him with innocent venom made by the 45
   bees. Returned from steep
Pytho, the king questioned his household,
seeking a child recently
   borne by Evadne – a
boy, so he said, who was
   fathered by Phoibos and
destined to be, of all men, the 50

greatest of prophets and one whose
line was never to fail. So he spoke, but
all swore that no one had seen, or heard of a
five-day-old babe, though in truth he was hidden in
    rushes and brambles, his
soft flesh bathed in bright shafts of purple and
gold that dripped from the violets   55
    growing nearby. So it
was that his mother chose
    this as his name for all time –

ep. 'Iamos'††! He, when Hebe the gold-crowned had
    given her fruit, went
down to the Alpheos one night and
    under the sky, from
midstream, called to Poseidon,
    his mother's father, and to the
Archer whose bow protects Delos. He asked for the   60
care of a people, and to him the clear, close
voice of his father replied: 'Rise up, my son, and
follow my words to a
    land shared by all!'

4. They came to the steep high
    cliffs of the Kronian Hill‡‡ and
there the god offered a two-fold   65
treasure of prophecy: at once a voice in his
ear not touched by falsehood, and later – when
    Herakles, sprung from the
line of Alkaios and bold in devices, should offer his
father a festival throng and the
    greatest of games – then, his

own mantic shrine at the   70
    summit of Zeus' great altar!

Since then the Iamid fame
    spreads throughout Greece. Followed by
riches and honouring valour
they ever walk in paths that are open, as
proved by their every act! But envious blame
    waits upon all who come
first in the twelve-lap race, for Charis   75
drips grace upon them. ...

'Hagesias' driver   † a river nymph   ‡Pitana   §Aipytos
**birth goddess   ††*ia* = violet   ‡‡Olympia

These mythic glimpses, unlike most, have served as a kind of
instruction in the victor's genealogy, while their sensory effects
have defined him as naked of any threat. An image of helpless
innocence has been overlaid with another of pure adolescence,
as a beautiful youth listens passively to a god who endows him
with mantic power. With these visions in mind, a potentially
resentful Syracusan audience will rest reassured, but this ode
was meant to be performed first of all in Arkadia, where the
victor and his party were probably to make a visit, before their
return to Sicily. And so, in order to involve this mainland audience more closely in the triumph of a man from the far west,
the singers insist on the local identity of their trainer and the
Theban source of their words. Taking a voice close to that of
their poet as he gave his instructions to Aineas, they seem to
discover a mythic connection between Thebes and Stymphalos
(84-5), while playfully suggesting (with the 'Boiotian sow' of
line 89) that sophisticated Arkadians may find this work coun-

trified, coming as it does from the 'countrified' north. They direct the chorus-master, Aineas (87), to recognise a local cult (88), their words in effect doing so, then to honour Ortygia and Syracuse, and this leads to a prayer that asks continuing power for Hieron, divine favour for both of the victor's home cities, and, for the chorus, a safe passage out to the west (92-105). To open this last phase of transit, Aineas' dancers discover an Arkadian cause for Hagesias' Olympic victory (76-end).

> ... If, o Hagesias,
>   your mother's kin, men who
>   dwell on the slopes of Kyllene,
>   have truly offered

ep. plenteous victims and prayers to
        Hermes, as heavenly
    herald and keeper of prizes who
        honours Arkadian
    courage, then it must be he, o   80
        son of Sostratos, who (with his
    thundering father) brings you success! A shrill
    whetstone sharpens my tongue and a
    flood of sweet breath comes, for my mother's mother was
    Metope, flowering
        Stymphalian nymph whose

5. daughter was horse-driving Thebe!   85
        Her pure water I drink as I
    weave an elaborate hymn for these
    spearmen. Rouse up your comrades, Aineas*,
    first to sing Hera the Virgin†, then to discover if
        we can avoid the old

98

insult – 'Boiotian sow!'– with true words! You
carry the Muses' dispatch and   90
   serve as their rod of
remembrance, sweet bowl for the
   mixing of loudly voiced songs.

Sound out the name of Ortygia,
   Syracuse, too, where lord Hieron
rules, wise in counsel, his sceptre
unstained! He serves Demeter whose sandals are   94
red, keeps the feast of the girl of white steeds‡, and
   honours the Aitnaian
Zeus. Songs and sweet-speaking lyres know him
well! May oncoming Time not crush his bliss and
   may he give welcome
with loving joy to
   Hagesias' festive troupe,

ep. come home from home, after leaving the
   walls of Stymphalos,
mother of sheep-filled Arkadia! Two   100
   anchors are best to be
dropped, on a stormy night, from a
   swift-moving ship. May some favouring
god send glory to both! Lord of the Sea,
spouse of a goddess whose spindle is
gold, grant us a voyage both carefree and short and
strengthen the joyous   105
   bloom of my songs!

˙leader of the chorus   †a Stymphalian cult   ‡Persephone

Hieron's potential resentment has been openly placated with a final stanza filled with his praise, but more subtly blocked by the central image of a helpless newborn child. In the listener's mind the ancestral Iamos is associated with a play of coloured light and a lingering taste of honey, so that today's Hagesias seems to be crowned, not with a wreath of wild olive but instead with a garland of violets. He returns from Olympia, not so much an equestrian victor in triumph as a youthful prophet of Zeus.

4

Celebrations for Rulers

Olympian 3; Olympian 2; Pythian 6;
Olympian 1; Pythian 1; Pythian 2; Pythian 3;
Nemean 1; Pythian 5; Pythian 4

The best known and most magnificent of Pindar's odes are those composed for victors who did not represent the ordinary aristocracy of Greece but were instead absolute rulers, or their close dependents. These commissions came, moreover, not from mainland Greece but from the two major cities of Sicily, Akragas and Syracuse, and from Cyrene, on the north African coast. Cyrene had been in the hands of one royal family since its foundation from Thera in the seventh century BC, but the Greek-speaking communities of Sicily were not so clearly defined as to their governance. Settled in the seventh and early sixth centuries by men interested in trade – sometimes drawn from more than one mainland centre, often second sons excluded from landed property at home, occasionally exiles – the colonial cities of the west were more mixed and more volatile than those of Greece proper. As trade increased, so did rivalries within and among them, while all felt the threat of a growing Carthaginian power in the early fifth century, and the result in the major cities was an assumption of power by the man who controlled the best-equipped army.

In Gela, a city on the south-eastern coast of Sicily, a commander named Gelo made himself master of the region, then annexed the rich Corinthian colony of Syracuse that lay to the north, destroyed it, and resettled it with men of his own. In Akragas, the island's other major Greek city further to the west, a man named Theron took power, and gave his daughter to be Gelo's wife, himself marrying a niece of the newly established Syracusan ruler. Then the pair of tyrants joined to seize the north-coast city of Himera from the Carthaginians, and to defeat the retaliatory fleet sent by that power in a battle that traditionally took place on the same day as the defeat of the Persians at Salamis in 480 BC. This triumph gave Gelo and his rebuilt Syracuse influence over much of Greek Sicily and at his death in 478 BC his brother, Hieron, was able to step into his place. He maintained the connection with Theron of Akragas by marrying that ruler's niece, and he enlarged his own sphere with campaigns in South Italy, where he defeated the Etruscans at Cumae in 474 BC.[1]

Within Syracuse Hieron was supported by his own army and dissent was not tolerated. Aristotle mentions the 'eavesdroppers' that Hieron employed against those who might be organising resistance to him (*Politics* 1313b), and a later historian describes this ruler as less murderous and cruel than the tyrant who followed him, but still 'money-loving, violent, and totally estranged from all noble simplicity' (Diodorus Siculus 11.67). He had power and wealth on a scale unknown in mainland Greece and in 476 BC he dramatised his position with a gesture that seemed to proclaim him as the partner of Zeus. The ruler of Olympus, at the beginning of time, had transformed a Sicilian mountain into a volcano by burying an enemy giant beneath it, and now the ruler of Syracuse transformed that volcano, Aitna, into the site of a city (an older population being forcibly deported). Hieron's son, Deinomenes, was designated as king, and until he came of age a brother-in-law, Chromios, would be regent. This act of foundation was, for Hieron, symbolic of his entire career and he marked it with a series of coins that bore an image of Zeus Aitnaios on one face, his own prize-winning Olympic chariot on the other.

Hieron's widespread power had a parallel in North Africa where the Battiad line had ruled Cyrene and its commercial empire since the time of the first Greek settlement. Nevertheless, in Pindar's time the king, Arkesilas IV, was confronted with powerful nobles, for the city's Greek founder, Battos, had arrived in 628 BC with two fifty-oared ships filled with colonists from the Lakonian island of Thera (Santorini), and descendants of these men had periodically resisted the throne. Taken over by the Persian empire in the late sixth century, the region had regained its independence and wealth after Salamis, but Arkesilas needed to restore his Hellenic standing. He founded a colony at Euesperides, just to the west along the north African coast, and then, hoping to attract mercenaries while reviving his authority at home, he decided to engage in pan-Hellenic games. His chariot was triumphant at Delphi in 466 BC, but a successful uprising soon followed and shortly after 460 BC he, the last Battiad king, was overthrown.

Where power was exercised by rulers like these the old aristocratic values necessarily lost their unquestioned authority. When both war and cult were directed by one man, athletic competition in particular ceased to be an aristocratic duty owed to the community. The members of a tyrant's family could not, after all, run or wrestle in public with lesser men, while games without them would have no prestige, and consequently local cults did not emphasise contest. At the same time, however, the rulers and their immediate families saw the equestrian events of the great mainland festivals as an ideal setting for conspicuous display. Strategic power was put into action in the mere embarkation of horses, jockeys, drivers, trainers and chariots with all their magnificent equipment, along with the ruler's own party, and a victory taken before a pan-Hellenic audience seemed to give divine confirmation to a ruler's throne. Gelo of Syracuse, when he won a chariot victory at Olympia in 488 BC, left his car there in Zeus' sanctuary, that the whole Greek world might remember his success. And when a Hieron, a Theron, or an Arkesilas took a prize it was marked by the magnificent court performance of an ode from a famous poet.

Arranged by rulers, such celebrations differed formally from those of ordinary athletes, as guests in greater numbers gathered into larger spaces to admire choruses that were more numerous (sometimes fifty dancers performed) and more elaborately trained. There were also significant changes in function, for a victor who was a ruler or a member of a ruling family no longer offered his supreme good fortune to his noble peers, to be shared as their due. He had no peers, nor did the *kudos* he had gained need any return confirmation from his community. He fixed his own fame and his enhanced reputation was imposed upon all aspects of a city that, like his own household, was in his possession. Odes made for victorious rulers did not, for these reasons, reflect the same joyous exchange of glory given and praise returned that regularly enlivened songs made for athletes of the mainland.

A poet, when hired by a ruler, had to meet the special demands of his autocratic patron while he yet maintained the forms and fictions of the generic victory song. Tradition demanded old-fashioned language and familiar musical modes, but since power was the exclusive possession of this victor, the listening group was not, as a rule, to be left with a sense of enhanced force. And since a tyrant's dependents had no need to remind themselves that they were not gods, the rulers' choruses were less prodigal in levelling maxims and self-deprecating jokes; they still pretended to spontaneity, but generally they gave up the trade-mark suggestion of error. Singers might still represent themselves as members of the *equipe* that had travelled to the distant contest, ready now to deliver an eye-witness report, but their actual function was to portray the correct (unenvious) response to a fresh demonstration of the ruler's power. Through these performers – or rather, through the words supplied to them by a poet – the community was allowed to announce, 'This is the sort of man that would fulfil our ideals!' while the celebrating ruler said to the members of his court, 'This is the sort of praise that my achievements demand!'

Moderns are often troubled by the fact that Pindar's most ambitious works served to strengthen men who ruled by force, but judging from the results, Pindar was not daunted by these special requirements. The victory ode was, after all, a much-elaborated version of age-old communal chants designed to put pressure upon supernatural creatures. The procedure was simple: using verbal repetition and the stamping of many feet, singers who represented a communal group identified a certain power as the agent of past benefactions, then asked for a repetition. A chorus might sing out, 'If ever you sent a fine harvest, send the same now!' or 'You are the same god whose property it is ever to uphold this city!' Herakles in Telamon's hall reminded Zeus of aid already given: 'If you ever have listened with favouring heart to a prayer of mine, o hear me now!' (Isthmian 6.41-3). Whatever the particular terms, the power addressed had to re-enact his definitional deeds or else undermine his own position, and this same magical constraint came into play when formal choral praise was given to a man. A leader or athlete, once sung as magnificent in battle, splendid in contest, or just in his rule, was bound to continue within that multi-vocal definition. Or such, at any rate, was the unspoken assumption of the victory ode, and Pindar gave it explicit expression in his Pythian 2. There dancers chosen from Hieron's court sang of that ruler as saviour of Lokris, guardian and lord of Syracuse, winner of limitless fame in battle, governor whose counsel is good, and then (before turning to court politics) they chanted a binding formula: 'Hearing this praise, learn who you are and *be* that same one!' (Pythian 2.72).

At Akragas, in Sicily, the court of Theron seems to have been relatively genial, and when that ruler's chariot won at Olympia in 476 BC, Pindar designed an uncomplicated ode, meant to be performed during a ritual banquet to which Herakles, Kastor and Pollux were invited. This is Olympian 3, a song that establishes a parallel between a happy Akragas made happier by the gift of victory and a blessed Olympia made more blessed by the gift of shade. Herakles is shown as a hero intensely aware of the mortal world and one who takes a gracious interest in men – one who can feel concern even about human sweat and exhaustion. He is a demi-god of fearsome physical strength, but his central deed here is explicitly accomplished with words of persuasion (16), and it culminates in an act of fostering which will bring comfort and consolation to lesser beings. True, the account gains a more heroic (and fairy-tale) aspect from its reference to the pursuit of the hind with the golden horns, the legendary Third Labour, but there is no hint of violence even there. Instead, the taking of this sacred beast is left untold, replaced by the hero's first glimpse of olive trees, so that the Olympic wreath seems to derive indirectly, not just from wilderness, but from Artemis, goddess of virginity and initiation. With an extraordinary unity of purpose, the song thus depicts a quality rarely attributed to the Greek gods, its transplanted olive tree standing as living proof of Herakles' sympathy with mankind, as enacted at Olympia. And meanwhile Theron, as he brings an olive crown from that shady place, seems to bring a bit of the same divine grace to the men of Akragas. Now his gift is delivered by revellers and received by court and community before the witnessing eyes of heroic powers who have come as fellow-guests to the ritual of the Thoxenia.[2] For the pleasure of this complex audience Pindar's singers perform an ode of rare simplicity.

1. I aim to please the guest-loving Tyndarids*,
        golden-haired Helen, too,
    while I pay honour to famous Akragas and
    rouse up for Theron the hymn of Olympian victory
        owed to the tireless
    hooves of his team! Once more the Muse
        stood at my side as I searched out a
    new-fashioned mix of Dorian dance with   5

    voices, to brighten our revel. These garlands
        fixed in my hair mark a
    ritual duty of joining the elegant
    tones of the lyre with a shout from the pipe and a pattern of
        words in due praise of
    Ainesidamos' brave son[†] – and
        Pisa[‡] commands me as well! Songs
    travel from there, god-sent and destined for   10

107

ep. him on whose brow the strict Elian judge,
    following Herakles' ancient rule,
      places a wreath of grey olive to
    bind in his hair – leaves from the tree
      brought long ago by Amphitryon's
    son§ from the shadowy sources of
      Ister**, to serve as best
emblem of games at Olympia, once his   15

2. words had persuaded the men of Apollo who
    live beyond Boreas.
  He made his plea in good faith, wanting a
  tree for the famed grove of Zeus as shade to be shared by the
    crowd and as emblem of
  valiant success. His father's altars
    already hallowed, the midmonth
  moon had watched from her heavenly chariot   20

  while he established on Alpheos' banks a
    judging of games and a
  most sacred feast for every fourth year, but
  no splendid trees yet grew in that field by the Kronian
    Hill – Pelops' domain.
  To him the precinct seemed naked, a
    slave to the sun's sharp rays, and his
  heart in that moment set him in motion,   25

ep. back to the Istrian land where Orthosia††,
    horse-driving daughter of Leto, had
      met him, come from Arkadia's
    ridges and glens, forced by commands
      of Eurystheus and by the

oath of his father to bring back the
    hind with the golden horns, the
gift of Taÿgeta, offered to Artemis.   30

3. Chasing that doe, he caught sight of the land
        lying behind the chill
    windblasts of Boreas and stood there in silence,
    stunned by the trees. It was a longing to plant just such
        trees at the turn of his
    twelve-lap chariot course that seized on him
        later, and now he is glad
    as, with the twin sons of Leda, he visits our feast!   35

    When he went up to Olympus, he left to
        them the care of his
    glorious contests of muscle and strength, and my
    heart bids me say that present fame comes from these
        horse-loving twins‡‡ to the
    Emmenid tribe and to Theron, for
        they of all men have most often
    given them welcome at their friendly feasts,   40

ep. piously keeping the rites of the Blessed! If
        water is best, gold the most honoured of
            all men's possessions, so it is
    Theron who reaches the outermost
        edge of success, moving from home to
    Herakles' pillars! No wise man goes further, nor
        even the unwise, and
    surely not I – only a fool would attempt it.   45

˙Kastor and Pollux †Theron ‡Olympia §Herakles **the Danube
††Artemis ‡‡Kastor and Pollux

This same Emmenid chariot victory was celebrated for a second time at a court banquet for which Pindar made an ode unlike any other, Olympian 2. Theron and the men around him were evidently acquainted with the mystery cults that were popular in South Italy and Sicily – Akragas was the city of Empedokles and held a sanctuary of the underworld divinities – and on this occasion the Pindaric chorus suggests that a blessedness beyond even that of victory may be reached by mortals who practise a benevolent justice.[3] The performance has three clearly defined parts, an opening section that fixes the supreme good fortune of the ruling house but cites the law of mutability (1-51), a central section that describes a different and surpassing glory that is permanent (52-83), and a brief closing section that testifies to Theron's candidacy for a kind of immortality (89-100).

The singers begin with a formal assertion of spontaneity, calling upon the powers of song to supply them with subjects (1-8).

1. Lords of the lyre, you Hymns, what god, what
        hero, what man shall we sing?
    Pisa means Zeus and the
            games at Olympia were
    Herakles' trophy of war, while for the
    victory won by his four-horse team,   5
    Theron must now be proclaimed! Host kind to strangers,
            prop of Akragas, scion of glorious
    forebears – he holds the city upright!

Zeus is begged to maintain 'these ancestral fields' (15) and this is a reasonable hope according to singers who produce a reassuring version of the law of constant reversal that must always shape mortal lives (19-22):

Pain dies, crushed beneath
joys that are noble, its evil defeated,
when the gods' fate sends bliss to its
heights!

The mythic examples of Semele and Ino are then cited, in proof that overturn may take positive as well as negative form ('Ceaselessly changing, high floods of pleasure and pain ever engulf us', 33-4), and on this note, the song arrives at Theron's family, which traces its descent from Thersander, a grandson of Oedipus (35-46).

ep. So may the Fate who rules over this   35
    family's prosperous fortunes bring grief to
    mingle with festival joy, then turn it away,
       as she has done since
    Laios' doomed son* encountered his
    father and killed him, true to the
    Pythian oracles heard long before.   40

2. Watching, a sharp-eyed Erinys brought
    death to his warrior sons† through
    mutual slaughter, yet
       when Polyneikes had
    fallen, Thersander‡ lived on, honoured in
    contests of boys, then in war – saviour and   45
    child of the house of Adrastos! Sprung from such seed, it's
       right that the son of Ainesidamos§ should
    meet with sung praises and tones of the lyre!

*Oedipus †Eteokles and Polyneikes ‡son of Polyneikes §Theron

Theron and his brother, Xenokrates, are like Thersander, warrior-athletes who uphold their house by bringing it glorious victories. Nevertheless, the first half of the ode has been filled with examples of mixed but inevitable reversal, which means that this present joy is necessarily unstable. The conclusion is inarguable, and so it is simply left behind, cast into shadow by a surpassing revelation. Even the greatest triumphs do not endure in this world, but success has another and unworldly aspect. Victory releases a man from anxious helplessness (51) and wealth can open the way to a transcendent existence, when it is used with a certain knowledge and in a certain way (52-100).

> Wealth, when inwrought with virtue, opens the
>   critical moment in every affair,
> rousing a deep and ferocious ambition. It is a

> ep. far-shining star, truest of lights,   55
>   if he who holds it knows what will come: how
> each helpless heart, as it dies, pays an immediate
>   penalty, then – for crimes
> done here in Zeus's realm – meets an
> underground judge* whose
> words hold a hateful necessity.   60

> 4. Through nights ever equal and equal days,
>   good men are given a
> life without toil, never
>   troubling the earth with rude
> hands, never ploughing the sea for its spare
> sustenance. Those who rejoice in keeping their   65
> oaths find a tearless existence, led in the
>   presence of gods most revered, while
> others know agonies past contemplation.

112

All who endure three terms in both
realms†, souls free from injustice,
follow the highway of   70
   Zeus to the tower of
Kronos, where soft ocean winds breathe round the
Isles of the Blest. There, petals of gold blaze
(some in bright trees on the shore,
   some rising up from the sea) and
these they twist into bracelets and crowns.

ep. Such is the rule of the upright   75
   judge, Rhadamanthys, seated forever
with the great father‡, husband of high-throned
   Rhea. Kadmos and
Peleus dwell in that place,
and too Achilles, thanks to his
mother, whose prayers had reached Zeus.   80

5. He gave a fall to Hector, un-
   shakeable pillar of Troy, brought
   death to Dawn's Ethiope
     son§, and to Kyknos! …

*Rhadamanthys or Persephone? †on earth/in Hades ‡Kronos
§Memnon

Like the passages of mythic reconstruction found in other
odes, this description of possible eternal life has become
steadily more specific, its images ('soft ocean winds', 'petals
of gold') more sensual, until with its final words it translates the
victorious Achilles from battle-field to flower-decked
paradise. This is the marvel that is witnessed in common by

Theron and all of his court, and it is labelled as such by performers who at once resume their opening posture of improvisation (83-end).

>   ... but
>   swift arrows rest in my quiver, ready to
>   speak to sharp minds (the mob will
>   not understand). A poet is one who knows much by   85
>   nature; those who need lessons
>   gabble like crows, cawing away at the
>
>   most sacred eagle of Zeus. Come, my
>   soul, take aim at the target!
>   Whom shall we strike as, with   90
>   gentle intent, we
>   let fly our fame-bearing shafts? Stretching my
>   bow towards Akragas, my mind set on truth,
>   I swear that no other city, in one hundred years, has
>   bred up a lord more ready to succour his
>   friends, less stingy of hand, than is
>
> ep. Theron! But, close upon praise,   95
>   noxious satiety follows, not with
>   justice, but fostered by envious men who would
>   hide the fair deeds of the
>   noble in babbling slander.
>   Sea-sands are numberless,
>   as are his gifts to his friends – who could count them?   100

The singers have praised Theron for exactly the qualities which might, according to the doctrine they repeat, place him with Achilles among the heroes on the Isle of the

Blessed. He has wealth and ferocious ambition, but also a generous sense of justice, as is proved by his choice of a song that promises permanent bliss, not to victorious rulers only, but to any man who combines these same qualities. Like the notion of reincarnation, the doctrine of separate fates for the souls of the sinful and those of the pure was known to various Sicilian cults, especially those of Persephone. (The penalty paid by all at the moment of death, line 57, is the one surprising detail here, for it hints at an existential crime, as if mortality itself were a form of impurity.)[4] Any one of Theron's guests might identify himself with the man who 'knows what will come' (56), and could at least attempt to keep himself free from injustice through 'three terms in both realms' (68-9), which means that this ode, with its revelation, adds a supreme item to the list of Theron's countless 'gifts to his friends' (100).

One more testimony to the flavour of Theron's court comes in the form of Pythian 6, a brief early song made for his younger brother, Xenokrates, who has taken a chariot victory at Delphi in 490 BC. The song is evidently meant for a youthful chorus, and it addresses not so much the victor as his son, Thrasyboulos, who has just come of age and is couched beside him. This may be his first appearance among the men, but whatever the details of the occasion, singers who 'plough the fields of the goddess of dancing eyes, Aphrodite' (1) turn to the son as soon as they have described the Pythian 'treasure-house of hymns' that belongs to the victor (10-end).

2. Winter's cold rains never will ravage that hall,   10
      moving from faraway thunderclouds
    in bitter ranks! Nor will winds carry it

off in a silt-swirl to undersea caves! Bathed in pure
sunlight, its portal announces, for all your
race, a chariot victory known to men's   15
tongues – your father's, Thrasyboulos,
taken in Krisa's deep valley!

3. Keeping him there, close on your right, you   20
     honour the law that, so they say,
   high in the mountains, the child of Philyra* once
   gave to his ward, Peleus' powerful son†, orphaned and
   left in his care: 'Revere, above all, the loud-voiced
   Kronian lord of lightning and thunder and
   never scant parents of due reverence   25
   throughout the length of their lives!'

4. Mighty Antilochos‡ followed this rule: he
     died in his father's defence,
   facing attack from the man-killing Memnon, the
   dread Ethiopian prince! Struck by an arrow from Paris,
   Nestor's lead horse had brought down his car and Memnon
   readied his powerful spear when, dazed in his
   heart, the old man of Messene called   35
   out to his son, nor did his voice

5. fall, unheard, to the ground for the youth, like a
     god, stayed at his post, to
   buy, with his death, his parent's salvation. To
   men of that time his gigantic courage   40
   put him ahead of all others in filial virtue. But
   all this belongs to the past! Today,
   piety's measure is most closely
   met by Thrasyboulos, who yet   45

6. vies with his uncle§ in rich display! His
    mind rules his wealth as he harvests a
    youth neither rough nor unjust but skilled in the
    ways of the Muses. Poseidon, Earth-shaker,
    master of all equestrian contests – you he   50
    follows with joyful mind, while for friends at his
    table his heart is as sweet as the
    chambered work of the bees!

*Chiron   †Achilles   ‡son of Nestor   §Theron

In Hieron's Syracuse, by contrast, the praise mouthed by
Pindar's dancers was more urgent and purposeful, for there
the ruler and his court recognised the bitter possibility of
civic dissatisfaction. Hieron was sung not just as warrior
(Pythian 1.48ff. and 72-80; Pythian 2.19) and lover of
music (Olympian 1.14; Olympian 6.96), but as a man
whose 'good counsels, more ripe than your years, bring to
each part of my praise claims unassailable' (Pythian 2.65-7),
and one set of singers insisted that 'no other man, more
lordly in strength and fair deeds, shall ever be wrapped in
the folds of elaborate fame-bearing hymns!' (Olympian
1.103-6). By those who performed the more intimate
Pythian 3 he was further described as 'a king gentle with citizens, open with nobles, a father to guests ... a ruler who
cares for his people' (Pythian 3.70 ... 85; cf. Olympian
6.93-4). And the same odes simultaneously proposed a
parallel definition of the Syracusan courtiers as a community
that recognised the presence of a superior power. As they
sang, Pindar's performers offered not only praise but obedi-
ence, while giving themselves mythic reminders of the
dangers of resentment or envy.

117

Olympian 1, made for the victory of Hieron's race-horse, Pherenikos, in 476 BC, is the earliest and happiest of the Syracusan odes, but even there a general warning is heard. His Olympic victory marks this ruler's power as superlative and part of the Zeus-made order that determines all things, and the singers first offer a version of his glory to all the assembled court, then engage in a mythic analysis of how one should, and should not, respond to favours from above. The opening places Hieron among the wonders of a gracious nature (1-23).

1. Water is best, but gold, like a blazing fire in the night,
   dominates all magnificent wealth, and
   if, o my heart, you would speak of
   athletic trials,
   look for no star in the day's empty air that   5
   burns with more heat than the sun! No other
       games shall we hail as
   greater than those at Olympia,
   source of the many-voiced
   hymn that embraces the minds of
   singers here gathered to celebrate Zeus at   10
   Hieron's rich and fortunate hearth!

   His lawful sceptre he wields in cattle-rich Sicily,
   reaping the best of all that is fine,
   feeling delight when the music
   bursts into bloom   15
   and we, like children at play, crowd round his
   table. Take down the Dorian
       lyre from its peg if, by the
   splendour of Pisa and Pherenikos, your
   mind is enslaved to

sweet thoughts! Unwhipped, he ran beside   20
Alpheos, lending himself to the course as he
coupled his horse-loving lord, the

ep. ruler of Syracuse, with royal power!

Pherenikos has brought his master into the embrace of power, and Hieron has called his court together to celebrate this Delphic consummation, but the song that follows produces a mythic meditation on gifts from the gods and the wrong and the right way to receive them. This it does with examples chosen from a tangle of Greek tales about sacrifice and eating that discriminate between mortals and immortals according to their proper foods.

The story was that Tantalos, a man who had dined with the gods and tasted immortality, had in an ill-designed return slaughtered his son, Pelops, and set him as meat before immortal guests. Demeter, in a moment of distraction, actually took a bite, so that when the boy was reconstituted, a bit of his shoulder had to be replaced with ivory. The eating of human flesh was, of course, a tasteless concept to set before Hieron's feasting court, and that version of Pelops' fate is ostentatiously rejected (52) by singers who offer two substitute meals in its place. They tell first of an innocent feast offered by Tantalos to the gods, in the course of which the boy Pelops was not eaten but instead ravished by a love-struck Poseidon (35-50), then of a criminal entertainment at which a presumptuous Tantalos tried to give the food of the gods, and so immortality, to his own mortal cronies (51-63). This attempted usurpation of divine prerogative brings punishment to the ungrateful Tantalos (himself already immortalised), and it also results in Pelops' expulsion from Olympus. This younger hero, however, understands how divine favour should be enjoyed and he asks Poseidon to make him the first Olympic victor in a scene that is mimed by the chorus towards the end of the ode (64-94).[5]

The double story of divine friendship used and misused, is told through a series of lively episodes in which repudiated events mix with others that are affirmed. Having announced Pherenikos' gift of victory to Hieron (22), the singers use Pelops' tomb at Olympia as an entry point for their mythic materials, and with a warning about poetry's deceptive charm, they at once announce that they mean to deal in novelties. Fundamental to their tale is a new explanation of the hero's notorious ivory shoulder: it is not a makeshift consequence of Demeter's greed, but a charming attribute that was his from birth (23- 30).

> His[*] glory shines in the
> populous city of Lydian Pelops, whom
> mighty Poseidon, the Earthshaker, loved   25
> even as Klotho lifted him up[†] from the
>   cauldron of purity
> marked with a gleaming ivory shoulder.
> Marvels are many and mortal reports,
> embroidered with fanciful lies, do sometimes
> outpass the truth, to deceive a
>   wondering listener!

[*]Hieron's   [†]at birth

One bit of the prevalent myth has been revised, but this was no more than preparation for the song's central depiction of two mortals who received supreme favours from the gods, one

to be punished for intolerable greed, the other to gain a further
reward (30-94).

> Charm creates all that is sweet among men; she brings   30
> honour and often she renders believable
> what is beyond belief, though
> following days
> make wiser witnesses. Men should speak well of the
> gods – less blame will follow. O son of   35
>   Tantalos, I shall
> spurn the old tales, to tell how your
> father once summoned the
> gods (as a favour returned) to a
> tranquil banquet in Sipylos, and how the
> lord of the trident*, mastered by lust,   40
>
> carried you off, driving his golden team to the
> high halls of wide-ruling Zeus (where Ganymede
> afterwards came, serving that lord in
> similar fashion).
> You disappeared, nor did those sent to search bring you   45
> back to your mother, and one of the
>   envious neighbours then
> whispered of fire, limbs chopped by a
> sharp blade into a
> bubbling pot, and of guests at table
> who, when the first course was finished,   50
> portioned you out and devoured you.

ep. I cannot libel a god as greedy of gut – this
      I shall not do!
   Small profit comes to the man who speaks slander. If

ever the watchers of heaven
honoured a mortal, that man was Tantalos, who   55
   could not digest such great
bliss. His appetite won him perpetual
ruin when, over his head,
Zeus hung a threatening stone, that he, ever
straining to cast it away, might be
   exiled forever from joy.

3. Such is the weary, unending pain of his life – a
   fourth trial added to three[†] – for he'd stolen the   60
   same ambrosia and nectar that
   made him immortal, to
   share it with drinking companions! That man is in
   error who thinks that his deed can be
      hidden from god.

[*]Poseidon   [†]immortality + hunger, thirst, strain

The ambition of Pelops, by contrast, was openly pursued
and properly mortal: he asked simply for his divine lover's aid
in a chariot race that would give him a bride (65-94).

Tantalos' son was sent back by the   65
deathless ones, down among
short-lived men, but when puberty
darkened his chin the lad thought of marriage –
that he might take, from her father at
Pisa, the much admired Hippodameia. He went one   70
night to the edge of the white-flecked sea
and, all alone, hailed the thunderous
god of the trident, who

faced him at once. Then the youth spoke:
'If Aphrodite's sweet love-gifts count in my   75
   favour, Poseidon, then
ground Oinomaos'* bronze spear and
send me to Elis
driving the swiftest of cars –
equip me with strength! Even now he has
slain thirteen suitors to hold off the day of   80

ep. his daughter's marriage. Great risks do not seek out a
   coward. Why should a
man who surely must die huddle in shadow,
nameless and nursing a feeble
old age, bereft of fine deeds? This
   contest awaits me –
give it the end I desire!' So he spoke,   85
nor were his words without fruit, for the
god offered fame in the form of a chariot
all made of gold, with horses both
   winged and tireless.

4. He† overcame Oinomaos, bedded the girl and
engendered six sons, each eager for
valiant deeds. Now, resting at   90
Alpheos' ford,
he knows the blood of glorious sacrifice,
there in his visited tomb close by the
   altar that all strangers
seek …

*the girl's father   †Pelops

At last the tale has produced an image of Olympian cult practice that fits the present reality and the singers cross in midline from hero to Hieron, praying now for a chariot victory (95-117).

> ... When fame is won where the courses of   95
> Pelops test swiftness of
> feet and painful endurance, it
> shines from afar and he who is victor knows
> honey-sweet calm throughout his life,
>
> thanks to these games. Bliss that each day returns is man's
> finest possession! My given task is to   100
> garland this man with Aeolic song
> cast in equestrian
> mode, certain that no other host more
> lordly in strength and fair deeds shall
>   ever be wrapped in the
> folds of elaborate fame-bearing   105
> hymns! O Hieron,
> god guards your every ambition!
> Let him not cease, and soon I shall sing –
> even more sweetly – of your flying car,
>
> ep. finding a friendly pathway of words as I   110
>   move beside Kronos'
> sun-covered hill! The Muses' most powerful shafts are
> nurtured for me. Men achieve
> splendours of various sorts but kings
>   climb to the peak. Look no
> further! I beg you may walk on the heights
> throughout the length of your time, and that

4. Celebrations for Rulers

I shall move among victors always as
poetry's manifest light, visible
   throughout all Hellas!

The final lines of this ode amount to a prediction made
in the poet's own voice – Hieron will have an Olympic
chariot victory and Pindar will compose the song that
commemorates it. He has earned such certainty with an ode
that associates the ruler of Syracuse with the victor in the
original chariot race (a youth who asked of god only what
he deserved), while it also issues an unmistakable warning.
To the courtiers gathered at this royal table to partake of
Hieron's glory, the ode says this: You are in the position of
Tantalos when the gods fed him on their own food; should
any one of you, thus honoured, repeat that hero's crime by
supposing that you partake of your benefactor's definitional
glory, making it yours to dispense, know that your punishment will be, like that of Tantalos, painful and never-
ending!

The motif of retaliation after an infringement upon superior power was restated in geographical terms in Pythian 1, an
ode made for a Delphic chariot victory taken by Hieron in
474 BC. This supreme triumph came soon after the ruler's
foundation, in 476 BC, of Aitna, his new city on the slopes of
the recently active volcano (there had been an eruption in 479
BC), and Pindar presents this pair of actualities as congruent
with Zeus' victory over the giant, Typhon, and his use of
Aitna as the punitive weight that keeps chaos inside the earth.
The parallel seems to legitimise unusually direct and explicit
praise for Hieron as the singers go on to laud his rule, the
'Doric' order he has established in his new community (61-6),
and the defeats he has given to regional enemies, with the

battles of Himera and Cumae explicitly mentioned (71-5).
Then, by way of choral advice to the boy, Deinomenes (designated king of the new settlement), the song seems to promise
a god-like and open-handed justice for the city of Aitna
(81ff.). Nevertheless, it is the force of the buried giant – and
so the supreme strength of Zeus' constraint – that the song
offers to its audience as immediate experience. Its music, like
the lyre of Apollo, creates fear as well as pleasure and the
opening image of the agonising monster resounds throughout
the entire performance.

1. Lyre made of gold, you speak for Apollo
    and for the dark-haired Muses! Dancing feet,
       splendour's beginning, obey you while
    voices respond to your signal as
    vibrating strings sound the opening notes that
       lead out the chorus!
    You can extinguish the immortal bolt of
    fire and bring sleep to the eagle   5
       poised on the sceptre of Zeus,
          swift wings drooping on either side –

    king of the birds! Over his head and his
    bent neck you pour a darkening cloud – sweet
    closing of eyes – and he sleeps,
    captured by tides of sound but rippling his
    liquid back. Even fierce Ares forgets his sharp   10
       spear as sleep warms his
    heart, for your musical shafts hold the
    wits of the gods in their spell, when
       aimed with the skill of Apollo
       and of the deep-bosomed Muses!

ep. But all whom Zeus does not love are
    stricken with fear by the voice of the
        Maids of Pieria*, be they on land or in the
    alien sea, even he who lies in dread Tartaros,   15
    Typhon, the hundred-head foe of the gods
    reared in the fabled Cilician cave!
    Now sea-washed heights beyond Cumae, Sicily too,
    weigh on his shag-haired chest while snowy
        Aitna, pillar of heaven and
    nurse of perpetual snows, pins him down.   20

2. Fountains of pure unapproachable fire are
    belched from within; rivers of kindling smoke
        pour out by day while, in the night,
    churning red flames send boulders rumbling
    down to the depths of the sea with a crash.
        That monster spits
    torrents that blaze with Hephaistos'   25
    power, a marvel most wondrous to see,
        wonderful even to
        hear of, when witnesses tell!

Such is the one who lies chained under Aitna's
tree-covered heights and its plain, his couch
    sharp as a goad to his resting back!

*Muses

Zeus' exploit serves as a foundation myth for the new city
of Aitna, and Hieron, by association, becomes a dragon-killer.
He thus has all the attributes of an ideal ruler, and the singers
portray him as a great warrior who responds, like Philoktetes,

to the call of friends (47-57) – one who has defeated Carthaginians and kept Sicily and South Italy safe for colonists from Greece (71-80). Then they seem to turn to the young Deinomenes with advice on the art of kingship which summarises the character of his father's rule (84-93).

> ... Reports of fine deeds not their
> own leave townspeople heavy at heart, but – since
>   envy is better than pity –
> don't turn away from noble attempts!   85
> Govern, taking your post at the
>   rudder of justice, your tongue
>   shaped on an anvil of truth!
>
> Coming from you, guardian of many, the
> least flying spark will seem great and
>   many will testify,
> for and against! If you would gain a
> sweet reputation, keep a fair temper and   90
>   never grow tired of expense!
> Let out your sail to the wind like a
> helmsman, my friend, but do not be tricked by
>   dubious gains! Only the
>   fame that comes after, sounded in
>
> ep. story and song, will announce how
> earlier men ordered their lives.
>   Kroisos' benevolent deeds don't wither but
> everywhere tales filled with hate seize upon
> Phalaris, tyrant whose bronze bull roasted men.   95
> Lyres and whispering voices of boys give
> him no sweet welcome to banqueting halls! A man

strives for success, then for fame;
    he who happens on both – and
takes them! – is granted the highest of crowns.   100

Through the exploits of their ruler, the men of Syracuse can
share in the violent preservation of order – the battles at
Himera (78) and Cumae (72) have been mentioned – but they
are to sense the weight of the punishment that will answer any
act of rebellion. A threat lies not quite buried in the strong
praise that Pythian 1 gives to Hieron and to his son, and a
similar note is sounded in Pythian 2, which was perhaps made
for Hieron's Olympic victory of 468 BC and misclassified by
Alexandrian scholars.[6] Whatever its date and festival, however,
this crown was taken with a chariot and team, and it is celebrated at length in a song that responds directly to elements of
dissent in Hieron's city. The ode is divided between effects that
are bright and others that are sinister and it insists on its own
mixture of forms, as its praise changes half-way through into
something like battle-song (69-70) because someone is aiming
slanders at the victorious leader. The performers will not attack
this outspoken 'ape' – that would be the work of a singer of
blame (53-5) – but they do insist upon their readiness to
support their ruler, should he be challenged (83-5). They give
voice to the loyalty that Hieron would wish to inspire in his
subjects, though to begin with they speak as messengers who
bring musical news from Greece to Sicily (1-8, cf. 67-8).

1. Syracuse, strongest of cities, precinct of
    Ares who frequents war's depths, god-chosen
      trainer of panoplied horses and men – I
    come from rich Thebes, bringing you song! Here's
    news of an earth-shaking four-horse

car that gives triumph to Hieron, keeper of chariots.   5
He binds far-shining crowns on the brow of Ortygia where
Artemis rests, for only with help from that
fluvial goddess did his light hand
    master those fancy-reined fillies!

The middle-aged victor is eroticised for a moment through
a comparison with Kinyras, a favorite of both Apollo and
Aphrodite (15-17), but a reference to his influence in south
Italy (specifically Lokris) returns him to his role as the domi-
nant power in the Greek west, where he has earned gratitude.
This notion brings on the negative example of Ixion, a hero
who, like Tantalos, misused the favour he had received from
the gods, and was punished by being fastened to a wheel that
whirled him forever through space (17-48).

            … Gratitude,
      rendered with awe, moves with the
    doer of friendly deeds. O son of Deinomenes*, you are
    praised by the maid of Zephyrian Lokris,
        rescued from war's devastation by
    your strength and standing in safety now, at her   20
    own door, her eyes free of fear! By command of the
    gods, Ixion is whirled all about on his winged wheel
    as he announces this law to mankind: The
    giver of bounty must be repaid with
        frequent and warm compensation!

2. That much he learned! As friend of the Kronian   25
    gods, he shared their soft life but could not
        support such great bliss – wits all astray, he
    dared to love Hera, whose place was in Zeus'

pleasure-filled couch. Arrogance
urged him to insolent madness and soon he won
matchless pain, created by two crimes of his, for   30
he first touched men with the stain of spilt
kin-blood† (nor did he act without plan),
    then, in the echoing

depths of the marriage hall, he tried to ravish the
couch-mate of Zeus! Each man must
    keep to his measure. Unsanctioned coupling
plunges a mortal into a chaos of   35
evil, and such was his fate when –
ignorant creature! – he chased a sweet lie and lay with a
cloud. She seemed the high daughter of Kronos, but what he
took was a trick, a beautiful bane of
Zeus' invention! He made for himself the   40
    four-spoked wheel of destruction, the

ep. prison whence he, inescapably fettered,
    gives out the rule he has learned.
She, the illusion, estranged from the Graces, bore him
one monstrous child, as odd as herself, who found no
    honour in heaven or earth. She
called him Kentauros, nursed him, and he then
mated with Magnesian   45
mares in the foothills of Pelion who
bore a strange herd that resembled both parents –
like to their mothers below but above, in
    torso and head, like their father!

*Hieron †he killed his wife's father

The listeners are all guests of Hieron, as Ixion was of the gods, and they understand that for them, too, any attempt to disturb the settled order of things would bring a perpetual bondage, while its effects would be malformed at best. The positive lesson about gratitude has thus been reinforced with a negative doublet, but before it defines the sort of ungrateful crime that it would condemn, the song offers an exemplary return in the form of praise for Hieron's benefactions.

God brings completion to his every plan –
god who catches the eagle in flight,   50
   swims past the sea-going dolphin and
trips up the arrogant man, while to
others he offers a glory that
never grows dim! I must avoid the bite of abuse, for
I see Archilochus*, off in the past, master of
blame, feeding on words made heavy with   55
hatred, but helpless! Wealth brought by fate-filled
   chance is wisdom's best aim, and

this you† possess, to display with free heart, as
guardian and lord of these fortified streets,
   and of your army! If any man claims that some
Hellene of time past stood higher in   60
wealth or in honour, he picks a
fool's fight. I shall embark on a ship wreathed in flowers,
singing of splendid deeds! Boldness, shown in fierce
battle, accords well with youth, and I name
this as the source of the limitless
   glory that you have discovered,

ep. fighting beside mounted men or joining with   65
    forces on foot. Now your counsels, more
  ripe than your years, bring to each part of my praise
claims unassailable. May you fare well! This
    music is sent, like cargo from
Carthage, over the silvery
sea – receive it with favour, a
Kastor-song set to Aiolian chords, gift of the   70
seven-stringed lyre! Learn who you are and
be the same!

    *seventh-century poet of Paros   †Hieron

Such is the praise of men who understand gratitude, but
here in Syracuse there is also an envious ingratitude that takes
the form of calumny directed at a ruler favoured by Zeus. The
singers have no talent for blame, which is properly the work of
a single and isolated voice (53-4), but they nonetheless
promise that ape-like slanderers and foxy schemers (72-6) will
be brought low by citizens loyal to Hieron (72-end).

       … An ape, among children is
ever found fair – yes, fair! –

3. but Rhadamanthys* holds power thanks to the
    blameless fruit of his mind, nor does he secretly
      savour the whispered deceits that
  track a man down. Speakers of slander,   75
foxes in temper, cause strong
evil to both sides, so how does their wiliness
bring any profit? Their work, like that of tackle, is
endless and done in the depths of the sea, while

I move above, untouched by the brine – the
    cork that floats over the net.   80

Speaking to men who are noble, the devious
citizen has no effect; he fawns upon all and
    weaves his own ruin. I want no
part of his impudence! I would befriend my friend
but as an enemy, wolf-like, would
track down my foe, sometimes taking a sinuous path!   85
Each order values the truth-speaking man, be it ruled by
tyrant or turbulent mob – even where
wise men watch over the city. No one should
    strive with a god who first

ep. raises the fortunes of one group, then gives great
    glory to others, but envious
minds are not calmed by this rule. Fiercely they   90
strain at the starting-cord, then pierce their own
    hearts with a painful wound, before they can
touch the goal of their schemes. Better, by far, to
take the yoke lightly onto one's back and
bear it. Kick at the goad, and you'll
end on a slippery path! May   95
I ever gratify good men, having my
    place in their company!

*underworld judge

For a ruler troubled by dissent from within his court, Pindar
has made a song which – performed for that group by men
chosen from it – formally voices an active loyalty. Everyone
knows that the ode has been imported from overseas, 'like

cargo from Carthage' (67-8), but this truth simply endows the singers with a more than local authority, raising their assertions to a level of general Hellenic principle. Their voices identify Hieron with the geographical Syracuse, giving him the local Artemis of Ortygia as a divine groom for his horses – she 'settles his team in its glittering harness with her two hands' (10-11). Moreover, they suggest a likeness between this ruler and a Zeus who, when challenged, is master of the perfect punishment. Plots against him will produce endless pain for their authors, while any results will be monstrous, like the offspring of Kentauros (his name means one who would rape the air). The warrior Hieron is to be judged only by Rhadamanthys, who never listens to lies (73), while the chattering monkeys who slander him will be hunted down by men who speak truth. The ode as a whole is an ingenious embellishment of the loyal citizen's resolve to bear the yoke lightly (93) here in Syracuse, where 'wise men watch over the city' (87-8).

A fourth song addressed to the ruler of Syracuse seems to have been made neither on commission nor for performance at a formal victory celebration. This is Pythian 3, so classified because, though no particular contest is named, there is a passing reference to victories won at Delphi by the race-horse, Pherenikos (73-4). Possibly the work was sent along with an ode that had been requested – perhaps with Pythian 1 – but however it was transported, its preservation suggests that it was given at least an intimate production within Hieron's closest circle. More than any other of his works, this song carried the voice of the Theban poet, but like all examples of the choral genre it could come into being only when dancing feet and voices obeyed the signal of the lyre (Pythian 1.1-4).

In style and design Pythian 3 is like a victory ode, but it is in one sense exactly the opposite, for its overt subject is the weakness, not the strength, of the man it honours. Hieron is suffering from a severe illness, and the major portion of the song is devoted to a fantasy in which the present performance brings him miraculous relief. This would amount to the assumption of a power more than human, and any interference with the work of the gods is dangerous, as proved by the linked tales of Asklepios and his mother, Koronis. Nevertheless, the poet takes his dream to an imaginary fulfilment before he finally rejects it, to end his song with ordinary mortal consolations piled one upon another as if in atonement. The opening words of the ode directly address its unusual occasion.

1. I wish (if the plea of all men may
     come from my tongue) that
        Chiron, the son of Philyra, still lived,
     though he is dead! I wish that he,
     child of Ouranian Kronos, ruled yet in
        Pelion's glens as a guardian beast
     friendly to man, just as he was when he   5
     bred up Asklepios, maker of
        strengthening cures, to be
     hero-protector from every disease!

     Phlegyas' daughter* had not yet, with
     aid from the birth goddess,
        brought him to term when she
     went down to Hades, struck by an   10
     arrow of gold from Artemis' quiver and
        dead by Apollo's design. Zeus'
     children are quick in their anger but she

paid no heed and, unknown to her father, foolishly
    promised to marry, though already
    mated with long-haired Phoibos and

ep. holding his perfect seed. Nor would she   15
    wait for the feast and the shouted
    gibes that young maidens
    toss at a bride in their twilit
    convoys of song. She yearned for
    faraway things, as many do –   20
    one tribe of men, the vainest of all, scorns
    what lies at hand to stare off into distance,
    chasing futility with empty hopes.

2. Such dread delusion belonged to the
    will of Koronis – she   25
      lay with a passing Arkadian guest,
    nor was her deed without witness.
    Far off at Pytho where sheep bleed, Loxias†,
      lord of the shrine, learned of it –
    told by that best of advisors, his
    all-seeing mind. Lies touch him not, nor
      can he be cheated by god or by
    man, whether with action or scheme.   30

Seeing her impious trick as she
entered the guest-couch of
    Ischyos, offspring of Eilatidas,
he sent his sister‡, raging with harsh force,
to Lakereia where the girl dwelt. Then her
    destiny shifted towards ruin, and
many a neighbour shared in her   35

suffering. So, in the mountains, a
    flame may leap from one
spark to destroy all the trees of a forest.

ep. Yet, with the girl placed on her pyre inside a
    wooden wall, fierce flames curling about her, the
    god spoke: 'My heart cannot   40
bear to destroy my own son in
piteous death as part of his
mother's sore grief!' He took a stride, tore the
babe from the corpse, and as the fire parted,
carried him off to Chiron to   45
study the healing of man's painful ills.

3. Those who came suffering from home-grown
    sores, those whose limbs were
        pierced by bronze blades or broken by
far-flying stones, others with flesh
ravaged by sunstroke or winter's sharp cold – all   50
    these he released from their pains! Some he
healed with soft chants, some with drugs to be
swallowed, or herbs to be bound upon
    wounds, while still others were
set on their feet with the cut of his knife.

Yet gain may trap science itself. Gold,
placed in his palm, bought   55
    even this hero – a princely wage
offered for bringing a man from
death back to life. Casting with two hands,
    doom in his fiery bolt, Zeus tore the
breath from them both[§]. From the gods we must

seek what is scaled to our own mortal
  wits, eyes fixed on the
path just ahead, aware of our fate.   60

ep. Ask not, dear soul, for a life without death,
  but of what's possible take the last
  drop! If wise Chiron were
  still in his cave, if sung hymns could prevail,
  I would have begged him to train a new   65
  healer of man's fevered ills –
  some son of Zeus or Apollo. Then, taking
  ship, I'd have crossed the Ionian Sea to find,
  near Arethusa's spring, my Aitanian

4. host who as king governs Syracuse,   70
  gentle with citizens,
    open with nobles, a father to guests!
  Had I arrived with two gifts – good
  health and dancers to celebrate crowns
    taken at Kirrha by Pherenikos in
  Pythian games – the deep sea once passed,
  I should have risen for him like a   75
    rescuing light, shining
  further than any bright star in the sky!

*Koronis †Apollo ‡Artemis §hero and patient

At this point the dream is abandoned: 'This cannot be' (77).
A god may walk through fire to transform a death into a birth,
but not even Asklepios, much less a mere singer, may imitate
Apollo's action. And so the song finishes, not with saving light
but instead with tired words (80-1).

139

If, Hieron, you take the point of old   80
    maxims, you know that the gods, for
each happy gift, send two that bring pain …

Hieron has known glory like that of Peleus and Kadmos, and so he necessarily knows a suffering like theirs (85-106). Nevertheless, while god-given bliss comes and goes, the deeds of certain men are brought to perfection in songs that survive. Even a god's son must live within limits, and even a Syracusan tyrant must accept sickness, but music can do what Asklepios could not, conferring permanence on Hieron's mortal achievement. 'Prowess endures in sung praises, though few find these easy to earn' – such are the song's closing words (114-15).

The heaviness of the odes made for Hieron is dramatically reversed in Nemean 1, a song that Pindar made for the ruler's brother-in-law, Chromios, who had gained a chariot victory. This man was the designated regent of Aitna until young Deinomenes should come of age and his song ostentatiously separates him from Syracuse through an opening address to Ortygia, an island sacred to Artemis that lies just off shore. Setting out from that place in order to 'build praise for a windswift team as a gift to the Aitnaian Zeus' (5-6), the singers would 'scatter splendour' (11-12) as they arrive at the victor's hall (18-22).

I stand at the gates of a man who loves guests, to
sing of fine deeds where a generous banquet is
spread for me, nor are these   20
halls without knowledge of visiting
strangers, come frequently and from afar.

Chromios is one whose qualities are manifest – 'Strength tells in action, wisdom in counsel, where foresight resides as a gift from one's fathers, and you, by your nature, use both, o son of Hagesidamos!' (26-30). Consequently the singers can forget the usual gnomic warnings and rejoice in a mythic episode that is entirely auspicious (33-72).

                    I, as I
     treat of magnificent deeds,
  eagerly seize upon Herakles,
     choosing the old tale of how, when he
  fled from the pangs of his mother's womb   35
     into the sudden brilliance of day –
  this son of Zeus with his brother˙and
     twin – he lay there in

3. saffron-dyed cradle-clothes not unnoticed by
    Hera, whose throne is of gold. The queen of the gods, with
    rage in her heart,
    sent down two serpents and they, when   40
    doors were flung open, entered the spacious birth-
    chamber, mad to stretch their swift
      jaws round the infants, but Herakles
    lifted his head, held it firm, and
      risked his first battle, his

    two inescapable hands seizing the snakes by the
    throat! As they choked, Time forced the last   45
    breath from their
    sinuous forms and the women who watched at
    Alkmena's couch were stricken with fear beyond
    bearing while she, the new mother,
      threw off her sheets and leapt to her feet,
    unclothed but ready to fight off the   50
      serpents' outrageous attack.

ep. Kadmeian leaders ran up in a throng,
    armed with bronze weapons, and with them
Amphitryon, grasping a naked
    sword in his hands and stricken with
sharp pain. On all men, familial misfortune
    ever weighs heavily, while
troubles that fall on another soon
    leave the heart free.

4. He† stood confounded, his fear mingled with   55
joy, for he saw the inordinate temper and
strength of his son –
the immortals had countered the messenger's word! He
summoned his neighbour, Teiresias, speaker of
truth and first among prophets of   60
    Zeus Most High, who revealed to
him and all present what fortunes the
    child would encounter –

how many lawless beasts he would slay on dry
land, and how many others at sea! He told of
one‡ who would choose
greed's crooked path and of the odious doom that   65
waited for him. Further, he stated that when the
gods should do battle with giants
    on Phlegra's plain, bright hair would be
grimed with earth under the storm of
    this hero's shafts! He

ep. promised that such mighty labours would
    bring, in return, peace and
unbroken quiet, enjoyed through all
    time in a palace of bliss,

where, with flourishing Hebe as bride, he would
   dine at his marriage feast, seated with
Zeus, Kronos' son, and praising his
   orderly governance.

*Iphikles   †Amphitryon   ‡the giant Antaeus?

Like Herakles the colleague, not the potential rival of a great
ruler, Chromios could celebrate his Nemean victory with a
confident song that asked his guests to stand amazed, like
Amphitryon, as the promising force of a newborn hero made
itself felt. When, however, an ode was to be performed, not in
Sicily but in North Africa, where King Arkesilas ruled over
Cyrene (Kyrana), a very different political situation was echoed
in the voices of Pindar's singers. In that rich city Arkesilas,
more merchant than military man, sat on a hereditary throne
that had been occupied by members of his family for many
generations (even under recent Persian domination).
Nevertheless, this legitimate power had been repeatedly challenged. Nobles whose families claimed antiquity equal to that
of the royal family had been on the edge of revolt in the late
sixth century and some had been banished. In the 460s, at the
time of Pindar's songs, Arkesilas was evidently attempting to
reassert his control by reviving the loyalty of his court – in
particular by assuming the glamour of a Pythian victory and
recalling at least one of the recent exiles. In 462 BC he
equipped an impressive chariot and sent it to Delphi with his
brother-in-law, Karrhotos, as its driver, and the result was a
sensational victory won in a field of more than forty contestants. Seizing this occasion, the king arranged for a two-fold
celebration – first, the public performance of a victory ode
during the Karneia, a traditional public festival, and second, a

grandiose court entertainment which was to end, so it would seem, with the return of Damophilos, a nobleman recently banished.

A Lakonian holiday that featured choral dancing, the Karneia provided an ideal occasion for the mimed portrait of an ideal monarch that Pindar designed for Arkesilas.[7] Speaking for the city and meant for an audience that included the ruler and of his charioteer, Pythian 5 maintains a tone of magnificence throughout, taking the first Battiad king as its hero and reviving that founder's contact with a healing Apollo as its marvel. There is just one, whispered, reminder of flawed mortality (54) in a performance that opens (1-26) with a worldly version of the mystical revelation of Olympian 2.

1. Wealth has broad strength when,
   mixed with clean prowess and given by fate, it
   comes to a man who accepts it as
   bringer of friends! O
   god-portioned Arkesilas, such   5
   wealth, mixed with fame, you have
   known since you first crossed life's
   threshold, granted by
   Kastor, the chariot-driver – hero who
   now, after winter's sharp storms,   10
   brightens your hearth with well-being!

   Wise men wear god-given
   power most nobly. You, walking in
   justice, have blessedness ever beside you!
   First, you are king – the   15
   prize of great cities is yours,
   as prince and heir, while

honour most high lives in your
heart, as your heritage! Now,
blessed again, with your Pythian   20
prayer fulfilled by your team,
you give welcome to these dancing men,

ep. Apollo's delight! While your
praises are sung, here in Kyrana's sweet
    garden of Kypris,
do not forget that in every event a
god stands above, as cause!   25

This unrestrained praise of the king is followed at once with
a passage like it in length and mood but devoted now to the
king's brother-in-law, the royal charioteer (26-53).

    ... Cherish Karrhotos as
best of companions! Not with Alibi, Afterthought's
slow-witted child, did he return to the
halls of the right-ruling Batttiads.
No – from his stay at the spring of Kastalia*   30
he brought the chariot crown and
    twisted it into your hair!

2. Twelve fast courses he
drove in that sacred place, reins never cut; he
damaged no part of the car that he
left as a gift, its   35
metalwork just as it was when he
passed under Krisa to enter the
god's hollow valley. It
hangs in the cypress-wood shrine

145

close to the primitive figure offered by   40
archers of Krete and set up
under the roof of Parnassos.

One must receive a bringer of
benefits gladly. Light from the
lovely-haired Graces rests upon   45
you, Alexibios'
son[†]! You are blessed for, after strong toil,
you are remembered with
praise even stronger! Where forty fell,
your fearless mind kept your   50
chariot whole, and from glorious
strife you return to the Libyan
plain and the city your fore-fathers knew.

*Delphi   †Karrhotos

Here a wise saying allows a transition to Battos, the founder
of Cyrene, as the fate of the royal line is cited as almost unnat-
ural in its consistent prosperity. According to local legend,
Battos was a stammerer whom Apollo healed and sent to Libya,
and from this tale Pindar extracts a magical moment in which
Africa, represented by roaring lions, is conquered by the voice
of a speech-impaired man. (Pausanias 10.15.7 preserves an
alternate version in which the stammer was cured, not by the
god, but by Battos' own cry of fear at the sight of the beasts.)

ep. No man is deprived of his portion of grief,
    nor ever will be, but Battos'   55
        ancient good fortune persists as it
    grants many things. For the city

he was a guardian tower, for guests, the
friendliest eye. Deep-roaring lions
fled him in fear when he unleashed his
outlandish voice, for Apollo,   60
founder of cities, inspired a dread terror in
them, that oracles given to
   Kyrana's lord might come true.

Next comes a passage of formal praise for the Karneian
Apollo as healer, musician, and sponsor of Cyrene's foundation
(62-81). Battos brought today's holiday, just as he brought the
first Greek settlers, creating the physical city and also its
culture, and he has passed his destiny on to Arkesilas. In this
present moment, the city's blessings reach their peak as buried
ancestors join with all citizens to applaud the king and his
Pythian victory (96-124).

      ... kings of old times,
summoned to Hades, lie
deep in the earth at his* palace
door, and their hearts perhaps listen as
acts of great courage are drenched in soft dew   100
poured out by dancers –
blessedness earned and now shared with
Arkesilas, their son,
who, with this revel, rightly hails

Phoibos the god of the   105
golden sword, for his is a Pythian
victory chant – repayment for wealth spent.
Men who are wise
praise him with words that I shall repeat:

Passing his age-mates in   110
mind and in tongue, he is, in courage, a
long-wingèd eagle, in
contest, a rampart! Trained by his mother he
soars with the Muses, while his
knowledge of chariots is plain to see.   115

ep. Each local gateway leading to glory
he has besieged and a god
   now brings his rule to perfection.
Grant to his future ambitions and deeds,
o blessed children of Kronos, the same
happy success! Let no autumn storm injure the   120
oncoming epoch with rough windblasts! Zeus' great mind
governs the fates of men that he loves – I
beg him to give an Olympian
   prize to the Battiad line!

'Battos'

Pythian 5 was performed for the whole city, but only men of
old family would attend the court ceremony, and for them
Pindar provided Pythian 4, a danced spectacle unlike any other.
Some have held that this piece was freely composed out of friendship for the banished Damophilos, or perhaps was commissioned
by him, and certainly he had visited Thebes, but the ode would
not have survived without performance, and this could have
come only at the king's pleasure. The simplest supposition is that
Arkesilas, having decided to allow the exile's return, asked for a
piece of great splendour, in the course of which a chorus chosen
from the nobility would urge the change that he had already
decided upon. He would in this way take on an air of gracious

accommodation as he attempted to satisfy pressures that had become too strong to resist. All this is speculation, but we do know what Pindar supplied – a kind of oratorio made on a regal scale but ending, after great complexity, with the sounding of one nobleman's name and the promise of harmonious quietude.

Pythian 4 is roughly three times as long as any other epinician ode, and it contains effects that are highly theatrical. The entertainment is dominated by the tale of Jason and the Argonauts, which is reconstructed in full vitality as scenes are set and impassioned speeches are directly imitated, and meanwhile the extended song pays almost no attention to its ostensible occasion. Exactly ten of its 299 lines are spent in formal victor praise (1-3, 64-5, and 256-61) and the contest itself is mentioned just once ('Apollo and Pythian judges have given him fame in the chariot race', 65-6). Finally, where a traditional ode would come back to itself and its formal purpose in the end, this one closes with a plea for the return of the exiled Damophilos.

Though they will stray largely from the conventions, the singers of Pythian 4 assume a familiar stance just at the start as, like an unrehearsed group, they present themselves with a prayer for inspiration (1-3).

1. This day, o Muse, you must stand with a friend, the
   ruler of horse-loving Kyrana! Revel with
       Arkesilas, and encourage this fair wind of song
   owed to the offspring of Leto and also to Pytho
       where, long ago, she* who
   sits with the golden eagles of Zeus
   did, when Apollo was near, name Battos as   5
   chosen by god to be founder of rich Libya!

   *the Delphic priestess

From place of victory, Delphi becomes the source of Cyrene's foundation (6), which at once takes the singers back into mythic time. The prologue of their drama is to be spoken from the Argo by Medea, the 'furious lady of Colchis' (10), as Jason's 'hero-companions' (11) pass the island of Thera on their return journey. With typical Pindaric chronology, this episode (9-63) precedes a major mimesis of earlier moments from the same great adventure which will occupy the central portion of the song (70-254), and the final effect is to absorb Battos and the local foundation-tale into the pan-Hellenic legend of Jason and the Golden Fleece, thus combining a story of error erased with another of contest and courage. With Battos as his agent, Apollo has determined the magnificence of this Libyan city and of its present ruler who, like Jason, takes on foreign opponents, and like Medea understands that human error cannot permanently block what fate has determined.

Medea is placed on the deck of the Argo among the Argonauts, as she calls out, 'Hear me, o sons of brave men and of gods!' (12-13). She has just learned that the token that ensured the foundation of a Spartan city in Libya has been washed overboard, but she insists that mortal carelessness cannot undo what a god has decided. The foundation of Cyrene must now take a revised form but it will surely occur: 'One day a root from this sea-beaten isle (Thera) will be nurtured by Epaphos' daughter, and cities beloved of men will grow where Zeus Ammon is worshipped!' (13-16). And to fix the truth of her words, Medea (her voice mimed by the singers) recreates the moment in which a disguised Poseidon (with a gesture mimed by the singers) offered fate, in the form of a clod of earth, to one of this company (18-40).

'That token of grand
cities to come, mothered by Thera, will be fulfilled –

omen received months ago at the   20
   mouth of Lake Triton when, in the
form of a man, a god proffered earth as a
guest-gift and hero Euphamos leapt
down from the ship to receive it! Kronian
Zeus marked the moment with

2. favouring thunder sent just as we hauled up the
   bronze-jawed anchor, swift Argo's bridle. Twelve   25
     days we had carried our seaworthy bark across
desolate dry land, following my advice,
   when that lone god suddenly
made his appearance, wearing the bright
confident face of a gracious and reverent
man! He spoke, using the language of
   friendship, such as a
generous host may employ when he   30
summons his guests to a banquet, but

we urged in excuse our need for return.
He gave his name as Eurypylos, son of the
   earthshaker*, Ennosidas, and seeing our
haste he scooped up some soil in his right hand, a
   happenstance guest-gift, and
offered it. Nor was it refused, for the   35
hero, jumping ashore, took the fate-filled
lump from the stranger's palm into his own.
   Now I am told that this same
clod has been washed from the
ship in the evening spray, to follow the

ep. watery currents below!'

   *Poseidon

Even a token given by a god can go astray, but fate at once arranges for its own eventual fulfilment. Medea announces that the foundation of Cyrene must now be postponed for seventeen generations, to be achieved then by Battos, and her final words about that future leader cross from the era of myth into historical time, as recorded in sacred inscriptions and family records (53-6).

> 'When later he enters the
> treasure-filled Pythian shrine, Phoibos with
> prophetic voice will command him to lead   55
> shiploads of colonists down to the rich Nile
> precinct of Zeus.'

Delphi recognised Battos as Cyrene's destined king, and the singers now hail him as ancestor of Arkesilas and origin of their city's prosperity ('See, even now, how Arkesilas comes into bloom … !', 64-5), but their return to the immediate occasion is only momentary. With the victory barely identified as taken with a chariot (66), they move directly into their major drama, which is to be the Argonauts' search for the Golden Fleece: 'When Minyans set sail in pursuit of that prize, god-sent honours were planted for them' (68). The adventure begins at Iolkos, where Pelias, a wily usurper, is warned of the imminent return of Jason, his exiled Aiolid rival for the throne (70-8).

4. What was the cause – what danger bound men to this   70
    voyage with fetters of steel? For Pelias,
        death was ordained, either by violence or by
    harsh plots, its source the proud Aiolids. An oracle
        brought from the navel of
    tree-shaded earth, where it was voiced, had chilled

his wily heart for it told him ever to
guard against one who would wear but a single   75
   sandal, a man come
down from steep heights to the
sun-filled plains of famed Iolkos, whether as

stranger or townsman.

The stage is now set for the opening scenes between the young exile and the throned ruler (78-167).

    And one day he came –
fearsome, grasping two lances and clothed in two
   fashions, his marvellous limbs covered by
native Magnesian garb while the skin of a leopard   80
   shielded his head from
shivering rain! Nor were the locks of his
glorious hair cut short – they shadowed his
spine as he strode, swift and straight, into the
   crowd at the market and
there took his stand,
putting his fearless purpose on trial.   85

Jason's sudden appearance is to be seen as like an epiphany – 'They knew him not, but stared while a voice spoke from the mob: "Can this be Apollo?" ' (86-7). Pelias, his lily-livered opponent, would drive him off with insults ('Which of all mortal gutter-bred hags let you fall from her aging womb?', 97-8) but Jason answers with firm moderation. He has come 'seeking ancient ancestral rights, unjustly stolen' (106), and pretends not to know the man who greets him so rudely (109-15).

ep. 'I hear that Pelias, true to his lawless and
   cowardly heart, has
taken these honours by force from   110
   rightfully ruling kinsmen of mine.
Knowing the violent ways of this lord, they were afraid,
and at my birth mixed their lament with
shrill cries of women, as if for a
burial, then, putting their trust in the night,
wrapped me in purple and
secretly sent me away to the safe care of   115
   Kronian Chiron.'

Jason asks the crowd to show him his familial house, finds his
old father, and is reunited with cousins and uncles through five
nights and days of festivity. Then he leads all his kinsmen into the
great hall of Pelias and the two once again exchange speeches
stamped with the plainly-drawn character of each, as if on the
tragic stage. This time, however, Jason begins, challenging his
opponent to a peaceable sharing of goods in which the usurper
may keep the wealth he has stolen but must give back the throne
(150). His key point is kinship ('The Fates turn away, should
enmity move among kinsmen and shame-bound respect disap-
pear', 144-6), and the cunning Pelias agrees, while asking what he
hopes will be a fatal price. The Golden Fleece must be brought
back from Colchis; he himself is too old for such a venture but
Jason blooms with youth (158); let him do this one thing and all
will be his! Sure that the trial is impossible, he ends his speech
with a promise he expects never to fulfil (164-7).

'Finish this task and
I undertake to resign both power and   165
crown! Such is my mighty oath – let Zeus be our
witness, ancestral god to us both!'

4. Celebrations for Rulers

So the first act of Jason's drama ends, followed by a passage which assembles the Argonauts and sets the expedition in motion, sanctioned by a favourable thunderclap from Zeus (170-202). The Symplegades are passed and the Asia Minor shore is reached, where Aphrodite supplies Jason with 'spells and magical chants' (217) that bring him power over the daughter of the king of Colchis, Medea. She in consequence has given him a magical salve, her promise of marriage, and information about her father's plans, before the chorus sets up another fully-staged scene. It is with the appearance of the king, Aietes (224), that the action once again becomes finite. This time, however, Jason does not speak but responds to a threatening challenge with action alone (224-40).

ep. Aietes then set out a plough made of iron, drawn by
  oxen whose pale jaws
 breathed angry fire as in turn they   225
  tore at the ground with their brazen
 hooves. Single-handed, he took them, yoked them and
 drove them straight on, cutting furrows as
  deep as six feet into the
 earth's muddy back. Then he spoke: 'When your
 king – or whoever it is who
 governs that ship – has completed this   230
  tillage for me, he may

11. take the bright Fleece with its golden fringe!'
 Jason in answer threw off his saffron cloak,
  put trust in god, and laid hand to the task. By the
 magical art of Medea the fire was made harmless; he
 dragged the plough back, fatally bound both
 beasts by the neck and, thrusting his pitiless goad 235

into their ribs, he accomplished by force the
   length that was set.
Aietes, agape at the
strength shown, howled with unspeakable pain but

Jason's companions stretched out their hands,
piled grassy crowns on his head, and hailed him with   240
   honey-sweet words!

With Medea's god-given help, the contest is won, the hero's
victory marked by the specific marvel of flesh untouched by
fire. The chorus proclaims this as the fulfilled aim of its tale by
first imitating Aetes' howl of pain and the gesture of Jason's
companions, then breaking their narrative to announce, 'I
know a short-cut!' (247). True, Jason must still seize the Fleece
from the jaws of a dragon 'more huge and swift than a fifty-
oared ship' (245-6), but 'time presses' (247), and so the
fairy-tale climax much loved by vase-painters is reached and
passed in half a sentence (248-52).

                That pale-eyed
   monster he killed with a trick, o Arkesilas, then took a
   willing Medea, agent of Pelias'   250
      death, touched Okeanos' broad
   streams, the Red Sea, and came at last to the
   land of the man-killing Lemnian
   wives. There for the prize of a cloak they
      tested the strength of their limbs,

12. then took the women to bed.

With one breath they have leapt forward to the return
journey, hinted at the fate of Pelias, and incorporated the fulfil-

ment of Medea's prophecy (50) about an alternate foundation
for Libya. Because of the lost clod, a visit to the women of
Lemnos is required to bring the line of Battos into being, and
with it the 'city of gold-throned Kyrana' (260), but Pindar's
singers race through space and time to reclaim the present
moment with a direct address to Arkesilas (254-61).

> On one fateful
> day (perhaps night) those alien fields took the   255
>   seed of your radiant bliss, and the line of Euphamos,
> sowed in that place, ever shows its perfection! In due time,
>   forebears of yours, joined by
> Lakedaimonians, settled the
> Island of Thera whence your race set
> out when, with honours from heaven, Leto's fair son
>   gave it the care of the
> Libyan plain and the
> city of gold-throned Kyrana where you now   260
>
> govern, devising right counsel.

Jason and Arkesilas have been paired as beginning and end
of the great foundation tale, both victors in foreign contests,
both ready for moderate yielding in the interest of order, both
favoured by Apollo. It is time now for the final plea, and the
turn toward Damophilos is marked by an extended wise saying
to prove that exile does not change a man's value – an oak
remains strong, even when felled and sent to another land
(261-9). This is an ailing city but Arkesilas, its 'most timely
healer' (270), is urged, while he has the gods' favour, to 'spend
your full zeal on Kyrana!' (276; cf. 290-1). This plea comes, so
he is reminded, from men who speak truth and serve as

upright heralds of the Muse (278-80) – singers who are at last ready to pronounce the name that will cap their unmatched performance (277-99).

13. Ponder the counsel of Homer and heed it: in
　　any affair, so he said, a good messenger
　　　　brings highest honour. Even the Muse gains
　　strength through an upright report. The famed　　　　280
　　　　palace of Battos – in truth
　　all of Kyrana – knows the just temper of
　　Damophilos. Boy among boys but in
　　counsel a hundred years old, he robs the slandering
　　　　tongue of its raucous
　　voice; he has learned to
　　loathe the author of arrogant deeds, while

　　seeking no quarrel with men who are noble,　　　　285
　　nor is he slow to achieve. Opportunity
　　　　makes short visits to men, but he knows it well – as
　　faithful attendant, not drudge, he keeps it company.
　　　　Worst grief, they say, is to
　　glimpse a fair deed that defies approach.
　　Yes, far from home and possessions, he wrestles with
　　heaven like a new Atlas, but immortal Zeus　　　　290
　　　　did once loosen the
　　bonds of the Titans, and
　　sails, as the wind falls, are shifted! With his

ep. cup of misfortune now drained, he prays that
　　　　he may sometime see
　　home once again, frequently
　　　　drinking with friends at the well of Apollo,

heart given over to pleasures of youth, or in tranquillity   295
raising his elegant lyre among
   citizen singers, offering
pain to no man, himself without grief.
Then, o Arkesilas, he might
tell of his welcome at Thebes, where he found a
   wellspring of undying words!

A lost omen will nevertheless come true, one set of heroic founders will be replaced by another, the fleece of the ram that saved Phrixos will find its way back to Iolkos, and an exiled nobleman can regain his place in Cyrene. When the name 'Damophilos' is sung out (281, opening word in its line) it rouses up echoes from previous passages which carried the same melody. With this exact musical phrase the giver of the clod appeared (28), and in fulfilment of its sign Battos was engendered (51), then addressed as blessed city-founder (59). Still to this tune, the long-haired Jason appeared (82), then mustered the crew of the Argo (190), and with the same notes clouds parted before the thunderbolt that sanctified the great expedition (197). This was also the melody for Medea's provision of secret knowledge to Jason (220), and for his subsequent yoking of the fire-breathing team (235). Music and dance have thus made sure that, when the noble exile is suddenly mentioned, his name will be heard as the echo and fulfilment of the many marvels that have created Cyrene. He will seem to be proof of Apollo's enduring concern for the city that Battos founded, proof that error may be transcended, and that Arkesilas' victory at Delphi at last brings some of the magic of the Fleece to Libya.

At the end of the performance Arkesilas will probably have signalled his agreement, and it is possible that Damophilos actually appeared. Whatever the arranged climax, however, the royal hall was surely filled with rejoicing on an unequalled scale, and in effect the king seems to have been momentarily strengthened. In 460 BC he went on to win the Olympic chariot victory requested by those who sang at the Karneia (Pythian 5.124), but in the decade that followed he was forced to leave the throne and take refuge in Euesperides, where he was eventually assassinated. His patronage of Pindar's Pythian 4 was Arkesilas' greatest achievement.

Conclusion

Every Pindaric ode was a bought product. Distinguished achievements were paid a 'wage' of praise, and he who made that praise likewise received a wage, as Pindar was more than willing to note. One group of singers suggested that their Muse's 'whispering songs, faces painted with silver', went out as prostitutes into a world where 'money makes the man' (Isthmian 2.6-11.) This was said in an ode made for an old acquaintance from Akragas (the Thrasyboulos of Pythian 6) who presumably delighted in a savoury metaphor, but the sense is generally applicable, for the victory performance was designed to provide a client with exactly the pleasures he wanted. Though audiences of the early fifth century took this truth for granted, post-romantic moderns sometimes find it distasteful, and so the inner rationale of this purchased praise must be reviewed.

While a victor shared food, drink, music, and the attendance of handsome servants with a group of friends, his danced ode sounded out as proof that his good fortune, though inherited, had also been earned through actions of his own. In buying a song, he had bought a witness to his essential quality, but this did not necessarily mean that his poet had supplied praise that was tainted or dishonest. In Pindar's view music was a divinely ordained expression of order, both cosmic and worldly. Apollo's golden lyre brought tranquillity, even to the god of war (Pythian 1.10), and *eunomia*, the balanced and peaceful political mode in which the archaic nobility rejoiced, was the gift of the same god who had given men the lyre, prophecy and healing medicines (Pythian 5.63-9). One word, *nomos,* could be used for a melodic line (Nemean 5.25), the regulations of a contest (Isthmian 2.38; cf. Nemean 10.28), or a city's constitution (Pythian 1.62), while another, *tethmos,* might denote the custom that commanded song after victory (Olympian 7.88, Olympian 13.29, Isthmian 6.20, Nemean 4.33), the rule that established contest (Olympian 6.69, Olympian 13.40), and also the ancient code that ordered a Doric community (Pythian 1.64; cf. Olympian 8.25, where it signifies the divine decree that fixed Aigina as a state friendly to refugees and strangers). The determined length of a hymn (Isthmian 1.62), the bit that tamed a horse (Olympian 13.20), and the moderation of a ruler (Isthmian 6.71) were all called *metron* because all were expressions of one principle, measure (Olympian 13.47). Games, powerful nobles, and princely rulers were all parts of a single brilliant system within which songs inspired by the Muses enforced a kind of discipline.

Because music was an essential force in this aristocratic world, the prospect of a sung hymn shaped the athlete who sought fame through contest. He would have to entrust his reputation to a poet for, 'though he has wrought fair deeds, if a man go to Hades without song, his panting labour is hollow and his joy brief' (Olympian 10.91-3). And a successful poet might judge certain deeds or certain men to be less than superb and so refuse to celebrate them, as Pindar suggested when he reminded Hieron's court that, 'Phalaris, tyrant whose bronze bull roasted men, is not sung at banquets by lyres and the whispering voices of boys' (Pythian 1.95-8). Actual blame was the burden of another sort of poetry (Pythian 2.52-6), but silence could suffocate an unearned or smirched notoriety as well as bury an action that was mediocre or base. The poets' criteria for musical praise were thus to an extent imposed upon the athlete, and furthermore when a Pindar or a Bacchylides did agree to make a song, he could (with the help of his Muse) issue a kind of imperative.

Through the chorus that danced for his friends, the athlete openly defined himself as one who had performed certain deeds, while the song used its magico-religious speech to insist that he continue in the virtues expressed by those deeds. Once he was chorally described as having certain qualities, a man was bound in faith to himself to continue in their display. 'Good fame', in Pindar's words, 'mastered' or took control of the man who had won praise (Olympian 7.10). The victor, moreover, had entered into this formal engagement before an audience made up, not only of fellow-citizens, but also of men of the future, gods, and his own familial dead, who 'listen with underground minds when great deeds are sprinkled with soft dewdrops of song' (Pythian 5.96ff.; cf. Olympian 8.77-8; Nemean 4.84-5; Olympian 14.19-20). Neither victor nor poet could afford to give off false sparks before such witnesses and so the victory ode was able, in principle, to fix the standards by which men of nobility (*agathoi*) defined themselves.

Just as he conformed to contest rules, the athlete who sought the glory that only music could give had to meet a set of requirements. A 'congenital fame' (Nemean 3.40) and a familial destiny (a *daimon genethlios*, Olympian 13.105, cf. Isthmian 1.39) would shape his life, but nevertheless he had to 'track down' the virtues of his ancestors (Nemean 6.15) – inherited qualities of temper and strength (Nemean 1.57; cf. Nemean 2.14-15) – and transform them into superlative action. Once recognised, the 'grand risk' (Olympian 1.81) had to be taken with a kind of modesty – one was its companion but not its master (Pythian 4.287). On the other hand, the man who would be sung could not be put off by danger, toil, or expenditure (Olympian 5.15-16; cf. Olympian 6.9-10), and he had to move only along 'direct paths' of open and splendid deeds (Nemean 1.25; cf. Isthmian 5.22). Victors heard themselves described as turning away from unjust violence (Olympian 7.91, Pythian 11.55-6, cf. Pythian 8.12, where Hesychia thrusts *hybris* into the bilge), and as using wealth only when that wealth came to them in rectitude, willingly, and without infection (Pythian 5.4, 14; Olympian 5.23), for noble souls were superior to riches as such (Nemean 9.32). They had always to look for the best in an active search, eager for trial and expenditure, but ready as well with approbation when the superlative appeared in the deeds of another (Nemean 8.39).

'If a man spends in joy, puts god-built prowess to work, and some Power plants a fair reputation for him, he will cast anchor, honoured by heaven, out on the furthest shores of bliss' (Isthmian 6.10-13). This was the model but, as he activated what was best in his nature, the man who would win sung praise had also to recognise the divine source of his success, for 'All the machinery of excellence comes from god' (Pythian 1.41). The wreath that was placed on the victor's head reminded him, his competitors, his celebrating friends, and men at large that, 'A man's valour is judged by the Powers' (Isthmian 5.11). A contest crown was taken, 'not without the aid of god' (Pythian 2.6-7, cf. Pythian 8.61ff.; Olympian 8.18) and this is why formal prayer (especially to Zeus) was so constant an element in the Pindaric ode, as dancers begged that present good fortune might be continued. The victory poet did not, after all, laud just the skill and strength of a particular athlete; rather, he praised the gift of glory received by that man from the gods (*kudos,* as at Olympian 3.39,

Olympian 5.7, Pythian 4.66), and he did so knowing that poets, like lordly athletes, were themselves the creatures of other-worldly forces (Olympian 9.28-9). Only with help from above would he be able to give the moment of victory a musical reduplication and – by moving it into the realm of what is remembered – rescue it from the dissolution that over-takes all mortal action. Music, *hymnos,* would then become an 'oath-bound pledge of magnificent achievements' (Olympian 11.6) – one that guaranteed the future as well as the past.

A layer of the population not only admired, but also scruti-nised itself through private rituals of this sort, saying, this is what we are – let us continue to be so! Such was the function of the traditional ode with its invocations, its lists of victory locations, its revival of ancestral achievements, its prayers, and its bits of gnomic wisdom sprinkled everywhere like salt. Pindar's Muse, however, was no ordinary artisan, and into this gold she worked an inlay of coral and ivory ('that lily-like bloom she draws from the foam of the sea', Nemean 7.77-9) – scenes from myth that brought bits of supernatural light into the banqueting hall. Mimesis of this sort belonged to the choral mode, but Pindar perfected a dramatic technique that caused myth and real life to meet for an instant in the eyes and ears of an audience. This happened at Aitna, when Hieron's court stood with Amphitryon to marvel as the newborn Herakles strangled Hera's serpents (Nemean 1.45), and at Argos, when friends of the wrestler, Theaios, heard Zeus make his promise to Pollux and watched as Kastor recovered his breath (Nemean 10.80-8, see above, pp. 27-8). Men of Aigina listened as Themis, speaking to the gods, blocked the begetting of a monster and in effect created the virtues of Achilles (Isthmian 8.38-49), and Hieron's court saw Poseidon appear to his beloved Pelops (Olympian 1.74). In moments like these the victor's experience of direct divine presence was replicated, so that all those assembled shared in the *kudos* that had been transferred, while they shared, too, in the victor's engagement with the future. The effect each time was like that of Zeus' eagle when it entered the hall of Telamon (Isthmian 6.49-50), for to a scene of organised revelry these supernatural intrusions brought a conviction of strengthened purpose.

Select Bibliography

For details of myth, see P. Grimal, *The Penguin Dictionary of Classical Mythology* (London, 1991).

Diels/Kranz = H. Diels and W. Kranz, *Die Fragmente der Vorsokratiker* (Zurich, 1985).

Translations of Pindar

F.J. Nisetich, *Pindar's Victory Songs* (Baltimore, 1980).

W.H. Race, *Pindar*, Loeb Classics, 2 vols (Cambridge, Mass., 1997).

A. Verity, *Pindar: The Complete Odes* (Oxford, 2007).

General discussion

A.P. Burnett, 'The Scrutiny of Song: Pindar, Politics and Poetry', *Critical Inquiry* 13 (1987), 434-49.

C.J. Herington, *Poetry into Drama* (Berkeley, 1985), 20-31 and Appendix IV, 'The Peformance of Choral Lyric' (81-91).

R.W. Johnson, *The Idea of Lyric* (Berkeley and London, 1982) 59-71.

F. Nisetich, *Pindar's Victory Songs* (Baltimore and London, 1980), Introduction (1-77).

G.B. Walsh, *The Varieties of Enchantment* (Chapel Hill, London, 1984), 37-61.

Scholarly works about Pindar

D.S. Carne-Ross, *Pindar* (New Haven, 1985), 1-39.

S. Hornblower, C. Morgan, *Pindar's Poetry, Patrons and Festivals* (Oxford, 2007).

L. Kurke, *The Traffic in Praise* (Ithaca and London, 1991).

H. Mackie, *Graceful Errors: Pindar and the Performance of Praise* (Ann Arbor, 2003).

W.H. Race, *Pindar* (Boston, 1986).

Works on Greek athletics

E. Norman Gardiner, *Athletics of the Ancient World* (Chicago 1987).

S.G. Miller, *Ancient Greek Athletics* (New Haven, London, 2004)

Notes

Introduction

1. M. Lefkowitz, *The Lives of the Greek Poets* (Duckworth: 1981), 57-66.

2. Cited by S. Barnett, *On the Study of Greek Poetry* (SUNY: 2001), 94.

3. Reported by Hallam Tennyson, *Alfred Lord Tennyson: A Memoir* ii (Macmillan: 1897), 499.

4. Cited by M.I. Finley, *Aspects of Antiquity* (Viking: 1968), 38.

5. For example, J. Irigoin, *Recherches sur les mètres de la lyrique chorale grecque* (Klincksieck: 1953); P. Maas, *Greek Metre*, trans. H. Lloyd-Jones (Clarendon Press: 1962).

6. G. Norwood, *Pindar* (University of California Press: 1947), 67.

7. Finley, *Aspects of Antiquity*, 38.

8. M. Detienne, *The Masters of Truth in Archaic Greece* (Zone Books, MIT Press: 1996), 51.

9. F. Dornseiff, *Pindars Stil* (Weidmann: 1921); W. Schadewaldt, *Der Aufbau des Pindarischen Epinikion* (Niemeyer: 1928); E.L. Bundy, *Studia Pindarica* (University of California Press: 1986).

10. Bundy, *Studia Pindarica*, 88, 92.

11. See M. Lefkowitz, *First Person Fictions* (Oxford: 1991), 191-201; A.P. Burnett, 'Performing Pindar's Odes', *Classical Philology* 84 (1989), 283-93; C. Carey, 'The Performance of the Victory Ode', *American Journal of Philology* 110 (1989), 545-65; M. Heath and M.

Lefkowitz, 'Epinician Performance: a Response to Burnett and Carey', *Classical Philology* 86 (1991), 173-91; C. Carey, 'The Victory Ode in Performance: the Case for the Chorus', *Classical Philology* 86 (1991), 192-200.

12. S. Orgel, *The Jonsonian Masque* (Harvard University Press: 1965) 108 cites a passage from J.A. Barish, *Jonson and the Language of Prose Comedy* (Harvard University Press: 1960) in which the masque is said to serve a 'society not so much aspiring after as joyfully contemplating its own well-being, the possession of the blessings it considers itself to have achieved. The compliments to the king … are one expression of this self-congratulation on the part of the community. To eulogise the king is to congratulate the society, of which the king is figurehead, for the communal virtues symbolised in him. To the extent that the actuality falls short of the ideal, the masque may be taken as a kind of mimetic magic on a sophisticated level, the attempt to secure social health and tranquility for the realm by miming it in front of its chief figure. The frequency of prayer as a rhetorical mode in the masques is hence not accidental.' Read 'victor' for 'king', and you have a fair description of the epinician ode.

1. Praising an Athletic Victor

1. J.S. Clay, 'Pindar's Sympotic Epinicia', *Quaderni Urbinati* 62 (1999), 25-34.

2. For a discussion of this concept, see L. Kurke, *The Traffic in Praise* (Cornell University Press: 1991), 204-9 and 236-7.

2. Celebrations for Boys

1. P. Frisch, 'Die Klassifikation der PAIDES bei den Griechischen Agonen', *Zeitschrift für Papyrologie und Epigraphik* 75 (1988), 179-85.

2. See bibliography cited in A.P. Burnett, *Pindar's Songs for Young Athletes of Aigina* (Oxford University Press: 2005), 185-6 and notes 1-5.

3. For further discussion of Isthmian 8, see D.S. Carne-Ross, *Pindar* (Yale University Press: 1985), 121-31.

3. Celebrations for Men

1. M. Poliakoff, *Combat Sports in the Ancient World: Competition, Violence and Culture* (Yale University Press: 1987), 68-73 and fig. 70.

2. For a detailed analysis of Olympian 9, see A.M. Miller, 'Inventa Componere: Rhetorical Process and Poetic Composition in Pindar's 9th Olympian Ode', *Transactions of the American Philological Association* 123 (1993), 109-47. On the mythic tradition, see G.B. d'Alessio, 'Pindar, Bacchylides and Hesiodic Genealogical Poetry', in *The Hesiodic Catalogue of Women*, ed. R. Hunter (Cambridge University Press: 2005), 220-8.

3. Kurke, *The Traffic in Praise*, 214-17.

4. Celebrations for Rulers

1. See G. Vallet, 'Pindare et la Sicile', in *Pindare*, Fondation Hardt XXXI (Vandoeuvres-Genève: 1985), 285-327.

2. On the significance of this festival for the ode, see E. Robbins, 'Intimations of Immortality', in *Greek Poetry and Philosophy: Studies in Honour of Leonard Woodbury*, ed. D. Gerber (Scholars' Press: 1984), 219-28.

3. H. Lloyd-Jones, 'Pindar and the After-Life', in *Pindare*, Fondation Hardt XXXI (Vandoeuvres-Genève: 1985), 241-83.

4. See S. Cole, 'Landscapes of Dionysos', in *Greek Mysteries,* ed. M.B. Cosmopoulos (Routledge: 2003), 210-11.

5. On Pindar's treatment of the myth of Tantalos and Pelops, see

W. Burkert, *Homo Necans* (University of California Press: 1983), 93-8; T. Hubbard, 'The "Cooking" of Pelops', *Helios* 14 (1987), 3-21; R. Drew Griffith, 'Pelops and Sicily: the Myth of Pindar's Olympian 1', *Journal of Hellenic Studies* 109 (1989), 171-3.

6. For an extensive analysis of Pythian 2, see G.W. Most, *The Measures of Praise*, Hypomnemata 83 (Vandenhoeck & Ruprecht: 1985), 30-67.

7. On Pythian 5 and its relation to the Karneia, see E. Krummen, *Pyrsos Hymnon* (W. de Gruyter: 1990), 98-140.

Index